# TRAFFIC SAFETY REFORM

*in the United States and Great Britain*

*

Jerome S. Legge, Jr.

*University of Pittsburgh Press*

Published by the University of Pittsburgh Press, Pittsburgh, Pa., 15260

Baker & Taylor International, London
Manufactured in the United States of America

Legge, Jerome S.
Traffic safety reform in the United States and Great Britain / Jerome S. Legge, Jr.
p. cm.—(Pitt series in policy and institutional studies)
Includes bibliographical references and index.
ISBN 0-8229-3662-3
1. Traffic safety—Government policy—United States—States. 2. Traffic safety—Government policy—Great Britain. 3. Traffic accidents—United States—States. 4. Traffic accidents—Great Britain. I. Title. II. Series.
HE5614.2.L44 1991
363.12′56′0941—dc20 90-49091
CIP

*For my mother,*

Jean White

# *CONTENTS*

# *LIST OF FIGURES*

# FOREWORD

Travel by private automobile is an enormously useful and consequential aspect of modern society. However, its ability to expand the radius of daily life with ease and convenience is achieved with regrettable costs, particularly in the form of the deaths and injuries produced by crashes. The need to contain and reduce these costs is an obvious policy imperative, to which Jerome Legge responds admirably in this book. Professor Legge also looks beyond policy questions to obtain further fruits for scholarship, in demonstrating important new methods for investigating the impact of social interventions and in explicating and testing models of the relation between law and behavior.

When we study the impact of social interventions such as changes in the law, the classic experimental method of laboratory science is often unavailable for reasons of practicality and morality. Social scientists cannot, for example, assign laws to jurisdictions at random for the sake of experimental control. However, social impact questions can still be studied scientifically with the use of quasi-experimental methods, which do not assume a manipulation of experience but which come close to the ability of true experiments to enlighten causal relationships. In the interrupted time-series method used in this book, past experience is a control for future experience; experiences at particular times and places are controls for experiences at other times and places. The results of these comparisons are powerfully convincing. The methods demonstrated here strengthen our hopes that social life is capable of scientific study and comprehension.

Analysis of attempts to reduce the toll of traffic crashes throws light on a central question in political science and the sociology of law: to what extent and under what conditions is law an effective instrument of social control? This book explores the classic mechanism of deterrence—threatening criminal punishment for noncompliance with the rule—in the context of drunk-driving laws. Analyses of laws regarding drinking age and use of seat belts probe a different linkage between law and behavior: the law, rather than modifying individual behavior, attempts to affect the environment so that the behavioral consequences are different. Underage drivers who would otherwise drink alcohol may have difficulty obtaining alcohol because of the law; and drivers crashing their automobiles may be more likely to survive because they are wearing seat belts. In these examples, considerations of morality and responsibility, which are integral to criminal law, give way to considerations of cost and effectiveness.

Professor Legge finds evidence for the validity of theory and the effectiveness of policy in all three of the policy areas he studies, though not for all of them under all circumstances. This is not the place to recite in detail what Professor Legge does so well in the body of his book, but I will note that the weakness of mandatory seat belt laws appears to lie in noncompliance, especially among the most dangerous drivers. The weakness of drinking-age laws may lie in similar considerations or in the narrow segment of the traffic crashes to which the countermeasure is addressed—those caused by alcohol and involving drivers younger than the legal drinking age. The weakness of deterrence-based drunk-driving laws is due to the difficulty of rendering the threat of punishment credible in the context of negligible probabilities of arrest and conviction. Professor Legge's work confirms the suspicion that threats may be better deterrents if punishment is certain than if punishment is severe.

Professor Legge's work deserves the close attention of all people interested in traffic safety policy. His message is encouraging: social interventions have a reasonable chance of reducing deaths and injuries caused by highway crashes. In addition, this work deserves the attention of students of law, who will benefit from his concise explanations of how the legal system functions as an instrument of social control, and of students of social science methods, who will see a powerful demonstration of how one can determine the effectiveness of social interventions.

H. Laurence Ross
Albuquerque, New Mexico

# *PREFACE*

Traffic safety was a primary issue at all levels of government in the United States and Great Britain during the 1980s. This book assesses the outcomes of government traffic safety policies in these countries during this time period. The results are encouraging, particularly in the area of alcohol-impaired driving. Laws passed in the early 1980s in New York, California, and Michigan profoundly reduced traffic deaths. Subsequent to the passage of these laws, a transformation in attitudes toward drunk driving became evident, especially in the United States. In England and Wales, the 1983 legislation mandating seat belt use demonstrates that dramatic results are possible if compliance is high.

While vast improvements are evident, there is still cause for concern. In 1987, U.S. traffic fatalities rose, coinciding with lower fuel prices, higher speed limits, and the repeal of several laws mandating seat belt use. If we are to continue to make gains in traffic safety, citizens must press government to pass and enforce safety legislation. Otherwise, gains made in combating drinking and driving will be offset by higher speed limits and poorly written and enforced seat belt laws.

Many people helped me complete this work. My colleagues at the Carl Vinson Institute of Government were especially helpful. I thank Richard W. Campbell for providing the funds to obtain the data necessary for this study and for encouraging me from the start. Barbara Newman and Patty Glynn were extraordinarily supportive (and patient) in teaching me graphing packages. It is an understatement to say I was not their fastest student and I appreciate their efforts. Thanks also is due to Karen Hewatt, who patiently and enthusiastically incorporated the countless revisions and rewritings of the manuscript.

In the history of writing a book, an author experiences high and low moments. Among my University of Georgia colleagues who were of assistance during difficult periods were Bob Durant, Arnie Fleischmann, David Ammons and Geneva Bradberry. Bert Rockman and Guy Peters of the University of Pittsburgh and H. Laurence Ross of the University of New Mexico deserve special recognition. Larry's comments and suggestions have been invaluable since I first started working in this area.

I thank my family for their support: my children, Jessica and Dean, my grandmother Mary, and my mother Jean White. This book is dedicated to her. Finally, I would like to recognize Bob Clute of the University of Georgia for the interest he has taken in me over the years, but especially at the start of my academic career, and for his contributions to our graduate program.

Of course, I alone am responsible for any errors in the manuscript.

# *TRAFFIC SAFETY REFORM*

*in the United States and Great Britain*

# 1

## *INTRODUCTION*

*TRAFFIC SAFETY* is an important concern of modern industrialized societies. While this topic has been on the public agenda since the massive use of the automobile and other motorized vehicles, interest has peaked in recent years with public debate on topics such as drinking and driving, regulation of the drinking age, and seat belt legislation. As with many other social issues in recent years, citizen activism has increased in this area. Largely as a result of such citizen involvement, many innovative traffic safety reforms have been implemented both in the United States and Europe.

The purpose of this study is to examine some of these traffic safety innovations. While my primary emphasis is on strategies to reduce drinking while driving, I also examine seat belt laws and drinking-age laws in a number of settings. It is my intent to determine which particular interventions or which combination of interventions are most effective in reducing highway fatalities. Based on these findings, I make policy recommendations, which I hope will further improve safety on the road and encourage legislation in polities that want to reduce traffic casualties.

Since the pioneering study of Laurence Ross, a great deal

has been written about programs to reduce injuries and fatalities on the highways.[1] Much of the literature demonstrates that traffic safety regulations have only short-term effects on highway casualties. The theory of deterrence, on which many programs are based, holds that drivers are reluctant to disobey laws relating to drinking and driving if they will be punished.[2] However, much of the literature demonstrates that punishment, even if mandated, is neither swift nor severe.[3] Its deterrent effects are therefore short-lived, because drivers begin to perceive, correctly, that severe punishment is unlikely and the probability of apprehension is small. By extending the discussion of deterrence theory and general prevention, this book hopes to determine whether any of the new traffic safety regulations have made a significant impact on fatalities.

## *TRAFFIC SAFETY AS POLICY RESEARCH: PITFALLS AND OPPORTUNITIES*

Traffic safety is a relatively new area of inquiry. Two reasons might account for this. First, research on traffic safety is primarily applied research, not basic research, and as such is not a priority among many academically based social scientists.[4] Furthermore, rewards in the academic community are usually more substantial for those engaged in basic research than for those engaged in applied research.[5]

Past research in traffic safety and the examples presented in this volume do not have as a primary objective the development of theory. For example, while deterrence is the theoretical concept underlying much of the drinking and driving research, social scientists engaged in this research are more concerned with the primary policy objective—reduction of traffic fatalities or injuries—than with developing the theory. The literature on drinking and driving demonstrates serious limitations to the theory of deterrence. Applied research on traffic safety is therefore handicapped, because basic social research has not yet developed a comprehensive or well-tested deterrence theory for these researchers to use. Indeed, applied research on traffic safety demonstrates the limitations of deterrence theory. Thus basic research is necessary on deterrence theory if applied research is to come up with methods of reducing casualties.

The second reason that traffic safety has been underresearched is that many of the regulatory innovations have not been tested either in competition with each other or cross-nationally. One might take the example of seat belt legislation. Several British Commonwealth and Western European nations passed mandatory seat belt use legislation during the 1970s and early 1980s.[6] While several studies show such laws to be effective, missing from the analyses is how efficacious such legislation is in comparison to other interventions. For example, in Great Britain, numerous attempts have been made over the years to reduce casualties on the highways by cracking down on drinking and driving during holidays.[7] While my work and that of Laurence Ross show the effectiveness of the separate interventions concerning seat belts and drinking and driving in Great Britain, little work has been attempted that looks at these innovations in combination.[8] Still unanswered is the question as to what might be the most effective mix of strategies.

In addition to Great Britain, the American states are excellent laboratories to examine various combinations of traffic safety policy. In the early 1970s, in response to the passage of the constitutional amendment lowering the voting age, many states reduced the drinking age. But in the mid-1970s, concern about the death and injury of young drivers, presumably because of their new legal access to alcohol, prompted many states to increase the minimum drinking age. Furthermore, as a result of the federal government's mandate to increase the legal drinking age or lose highway funds, nearly all states raised the legal age for alcohol consumption by 1987.

Simultaneously, the drinking and driving issue arrived on the public agenda. Interest groups such as Mothers Against Drunk Driving (MADD) and church and civic groups began to press for the reform of laws governing the drinking driver. Concern was expressed both for the high toll of death and injury on U.S. highways due to alcohol and the uneven, casual, and sometimes absent enforcement of existing laws. As a result, the U.S. states passed a variety of new laws governing drinking and driving. Most of this legislation standardized punishment, including minimum fines, and many increased the penalty imposed on to the drinking driver, especially for second and third offenses. On these occasions, the law often mandates the sentence.

The most recent area of reform at the state level is seat belt legislation. The first mandatory seat belt use law in the United States went into effect in New York State in January 1985. Later, many other states followed suit. Evidence is still accumulating on the effectiveness of these laws, and research has barely touched the consequences of the vast amount of traffic safety legislation passed in the states, either individually or in combination.[9]

Except for work on drinking and driving legislation, there has been very little research explicitly comparing the effectiveness of recent state laws with each other or with other nations. Essentially, three strategies have been used: raising the drinking age; passing stricter and, in most cases, more punitive laws to regulate drinking and driving; and most recently, passing seat belt legislation. In terms of drinking-age legislation, many state laws differ. For example, Michigan abruptly raised the drinking age from eighteen to twenty-one, while Georgia has taken a more incremental approach by raising the age a year at a time.[10] With regard to drunk driving, nearly all states passed some legislation during the early 1980s, but here, too, there is considerable variation.[11] For instance, roughly half the states mandate a jail sentence in the case of second or third offenses (a few states, such as Maine, for the first infraction).[12] In such cases, the laws cause problems in the legal system, such as a decline in guilty pleas, jail overcrowding, and judicial reluctance to carry out sentencing. There is little evidence of permanent deterrent effects from such laws; rather, deterrence appears linked more closely with the certainty and swiftness of the law rather than its severity.[13]

On the most recent strategy, the mandatory use of seat belts, there is considerable variation among the states as well. By the end of 1988, twenty-nine states had passed seat belt laws, largely in response to a directive from the U.S. Department of Transportation. Under DOT regulations, air bags are required for automobiles beginning with 1990 models, partially because two-thirds of the U.S. population was not covered by mandatory seat belt use laws by 1989. Implementation of the air bag law will be gradual, beginning with three million cars. Since the regulation relating air bags to seat belt legislation was issued in 1984, many state legislatures passed laws, but by the end of 1987, the momentum was lost. Two states, Nebraska and Massachusetts, which had earlier mandated seat belt use, repealed their laws by popular referenda in the November 1986 election. In short, because of the variety of legislation, American states make interesting laboratories for social science research.

## *CASE STUDIES*

This book examines policy interventions to improve traffic safety in the United States and Great Britain. It compares several states with each other and with Great Britain. The states selected are New York, California, and Michigan. Traditional analysis of traffic safety is comparative and involves nations primarily outside the United States, especially British Commonwealth countries; as Franklin Zimring indicates, "Drunk driving is . . . a domestic political concern that increasingly operates from a transnational data base."[14] The recent experience of many states adds a new dimension to the comparative framework.

The three states were chosen because they are large industrial states and thus are comparable to Britain and to each other. Also, they all have extensive road systems with high utilization. Further, these states are among the leaders in citizen activism and policy innovations in traffic safety. For example, all three states were at the forefront of seat belt legislation, with New York being the first to pass such a law. All three took innovative steps to combat drinking and driving in the early 1980s, with particular emphasis on increasing the certainty and swiftness of punishment.

But there are major differences as well. Through the early 1970s, New York was among the few states that permitted the consumption of all alcohol (liquor, wine, and beer) at age eighteen. In 1982 the drinking age was raised to nineteen, and in 1985, due in large part to pressure from the federal government, the age was raised to twenty-one. Michigan took a more sweeping approach, raising the age from eighteen to twenty-one in 1978. In California, the age has been maintained at twenty-one. Also, there are differences in seat belt laws. New York has primary enforcement, where a motorist can be issued a citation for simply not wearing the belt (as in Britain); California and Michigan are secondary enforcement states, where it is necessary to commit another violation to be cited for violation of the seat belt law.

Great Britain, like the three states, has been active in traffic safety policy. It was one of the first nations to use breath and chemical tests systematically to reduce highway fatalities and injuries.[15] In addition, while its implementation of seat belt legislation occurred after such laws were passed in other European and British Commonwealth nations, the legislation became effective just prior to the U.S. (31 January 1983). Also, over the years attempts have been made to control drinking and driving through legal and administrative approaches. The British case differs from the American on the age variable. The mimimum age for the consumption of alcohol in Britain is eighteen, and there have been no legislative attempts to tamper with this regulation. While those who lobbied for reform no doubt had a variety of goals in mind in their advocacy (e.g., retribution and legal punishment in the case of drunk drivers or the limitation of alcohol availability in general), one ultimate goal agreed upon was fatality reduction.

The cases chosen present a mix of strategies. Administrative or legal attempts to deter drunk driving took the following forms in three U.S. states and Great Britain.

- New York: primary enforcement of seat belt legislation; change in minimum drinking age was least abrupt.
- California: secondary enforcement of seat belt legislation; minimum drinking age kept at twenty-one.
- Michigan: secondary enforcement of seat belt legislation; minimum drinking age was most abrupt.
- Great Britain: primary enforcement of seat belt legislation; minimum drinking age kept at eighteen.

I hope that the variety of innovations included in this study will enable specification of the most effective approaches to highway safety and the options open to decision makers.

## *THE APPROACH OF THE BOOK*

The next two chapters establish the theoretical and methodological foundations of this book. The literature on drinking and driving is cast in the framework of deterrence theory, while changing the drinking age and mandating seat belts fit more into a strategy of long-term prevention. The hypotheses employ the theoretical framework of Zimring and Hawkins. The book argues that attempts to change behavior in traffic safety are similar to changing customs in other areas of human behavior.[16] Since the custom of drinking and driving is the most difficult to change, I hypothesize that laws to deter such behavior will be effective primarily in the short run. Alternatively, because seat belt laws and drinking-age laws are integrated more generally with long-term societal goals of health and safety, we might expect a more permanent reduction in fatalities from these interventions. Indeed, these latter interventions have helped to maintain the initial gains of drinking and driving legislation for extended time periods.[17]

Chapter 3 presents the methodology of this study—interrupted time-series analysis—and describes the dependent variable of focus—the traffic fatality. The interrupted time-series technique examines the behavior of the dependent variable in response to the different policy interventions over time.[18]

Normally, the case is strengthened if a control unit is used that did not receive an intervention. This design is difficult with the U.S. states, as nearly all of them implemented at least one of the interventions considered. However, control is attempted through the use of nonequivalent dependent variables. For example, there are some periods during which we might expect drinking and driving legislation to have an especially strong effect (such as nights and weekends). At other times, such laws may have only small impacts (such as daytime hours).

Chapters 4 through 7 test the effectiveness of the policy interventions, using interrupted time-series techniques. In addition to data analysis, the historical development of the innovations, the policy setting, the implementation of the interventions and, finally, compliance are discussed. Implementation and compliance are especially crucial issues, for one might not expect the laws to have any significant impact if they are not obeyed or enforced. For example, the British seat belt law has demonstrated a compliance of over 95 percent since its effective date, while surveys in the states show a much lower level of adherence to the law.[19]

Chapter 8 brings all four cases into systematic comparison, describes the strengths and flaws of different innovations and discusses the implications of the findings for policy makers.

# 2

## *DETERRENCE THEORY AND GENERAL PREVENTION: THE DEVELOPMENT OF HYPOTHESES*

*THE LOGIC* of legislation and policy development in the traffic safety field has depended largely on deterrence theory. While this theory has become more complex in recent years, its basic proposition holds that people are less likely to violate a law if they face criminal sanction. Traditionally, the theory posits that the more severe the punishment, the less likely that the person will violate legal norms. In more recent years, the theory includes swiftness and certainty of punishment to make deterrence effective.

While deterrence in traffic safety is aimed primarily at preventing drinking and driving, its logic extends to seat belt requirements and observing the legal drinking age.[1] In terms of punitive measures to alter behavior, however, deterrence has limitations with regard to these two policies. Legal punishment for underage drinking in most states focuses on the supplier of the alcohol as opposed to the consumer; for disregard of the seat belt law, legal penalties are minimal, especially in states with secondary enforcement. Rather than fitting into the literature of deterrence, as drinking and driving laws do, seat belt laws and drinking-age laws are more aptly classified under general prevention.[2] This concept might be thought of as a long-term strategy to improve health or safety, which involves changing public attitudes or life styles rather than punishing a crime.

In this chapter, I discuss the most recent literature in the fields of deterrence and general prevention, beginning with deterrence, with reference to criminal activities, and then move to its application to traffic safety. Based upon this literature review, I formulate the hypotheses.

## *DETERRENCE AND CRIMINAL ACTIVITY*

### *Attitudinal and Perceptual Studies*

The best that might be said of deterrence theory as it applies to criminal justice is that findings are mixed. The answer to the question whether deterrence works at all depends on the nature of the crime under consideration, the circumstances under which it occurs, and the characteristics of the people committing the crime. In short, with the individual as the unit of analysis in attitudinal studies, the outcome of the dependent variable most often is conditional. For example, one of the earlier studies of the use of deterrence for parking violations states that is important to distinguish between

> those circumstances under which particular types of punishment do in fact act as a deterrent and those circumstances under which particular types of punishment have little or no effect. It is naive to suppose that punishment exists in a vacuum and is unrelated to the specific kinds of acts and the meaning which punishment has for the actor.[3]

Further, deterrence sometimes functions in ways that has no relationship to the law and thus is very difficult for society to regulate. For example, "a specific and unique deterrence effect" manifests itself among many youths when they reach age sixteen, because legal sanctions for punishment at that age have much more serious consequences.[4] While it might be argued that government could lower the age of accountability, many citizens may find this morally or ethically unacceptable.

Nevertheless, research demonstrates some areas of criminal justice where the concept of deterrence seems to work. For example, the extent to which the juvenile justice system is likely to discourage further criminality by delinquents is influenced by the type of court these delinquents experience initially.[5] One study, after examining survey data from Arizona high school students, poses the normative erosion hypothesis, which holds that, if courts are lenient with juvenile offenders and take a hands-off approach to punishment, perception of the seriousness of the crime by the juvenile may be eroded. Thus, further crime may be encouraged. (This work does not address the issue of whether more punitive courts are successful in increasing offenders' negative attitudes toward delinquency.)

Surveys of juveniles cast some doubt on the above findings.[6] Neither perceived certainty, severity, nor swiftness of punishment is related to student misbehavior; however, swiftness of punishment does have a significant effect on fear of punishment. Thus, the threat of more severe legal sanctions seems to influence neither behavior nor fear, a finding consistent with most literature on traffic safety, probably because of the correct perception of low probability of apprehension. For this reason, swiftness of punishment is increasingly advocated over severity of punishment in the traffic safety literature.[7]

The limitations of deterrence for juveniles are supported by similar studies of adult offenders. For example, criminal behavior in adults is associated only weakly with perceived threat of punishment.[8] Instead, other social and behavioral factors (education, offense histories, and perceptions regarding immunity from punishment) are more important. For experienced offenders, punishment has no substantial effect on perceived threat. Furthermore, "punishment may actually lower perceived threat by increasing approval of criminal behavior."[9] In contrast, for naive offenders, punishment does increase the perception of threat. The reason is that, once inside the criminal justice system, the seasoned offender has fewer costs to pay if apprehended for a crime, because incarceration is likely to be longer and parole remote.

The above findings are further supported by a rational choice model of deterrence.[10] Contending that many prior studies of deterrence focus on noncriminal populations and pay little attention to the reward structure of individual-level decision making on criminality, this study tests the rational choice model on individual criminals at high risk for legal sanction. While the reward component of the model is supported, the deterrence or cost component fails to uncover any substantive or statistical significance of perceived risk of formal sanction.

Thus far, studies that use the individual as the unit of analysis do not offer firm and consistent support for the deterrence hypothesis. The one area of criminal behavior supporting the hypothesis is domestic violence. Data from an experiment sponsored by the Police Foundation and the Minneapolis Police Department were used to examine three possible courses of action by the police in the event of domestic assault: arrest, advice (including mediation), and an order for the suspect to leave the home for eight hours.[11] These treatments were decided on a random basis and the suspects were followed for six months after police intervention. The analysis convincingly demonstrates that the most severe intervention, arrest, was the most successful. Those arrested subsequently engaged in domestic violence to a much lesser extent than those in the other categories. Furthermore, the effects of arrest were also efficacious for those persons with a prior criminal history and past incidents of domestic violence. This finding casts some doubt on the assertion of other studies—that the most severe offenders are not deterred, because the crime is looked upon with approval rather than with condemnation.

A more recent study supports the Minneapolis findings, although the research design is somewhat weaker.[12] Using California data on 783 incidents of wife battery, the analysis over a twenty-eight-month period reveals that those arrested (207) tend to be involved in fewer subsequent cases of spousal abuse. Further, the incidence of crime is greatest for those normally most at risk for future violations, including those with prior criminal records and past episodes of wife battery.

### *Studies at the Aggregate Level*

In general, results are weaker when deterrence is analyzed with aggregate-level data. To begin, there is little evidence that enforcement of specific laws reduces crime. Conceptual problems are involved in ascertaining whether criminals are deterred by arrests or if the police respond to increases in crime.[13] Regression analysis used both rates and raw numbers in equations for homicide, robbery, and burglary. Contrary to the theory of deterrence, arrests do follow crimes. The commonsense proposition that the perception of arrest by criminals is a deterrent to crime must be reexamined.

A substantial amount of research evaluates the impact of legal control of firearms. The Massachusetts Gun Control Law specifies a one-year prison sentence for illegal firearm possession. Three categories of crime—homicide, armed robbery, and other crimes committed with a gun—reveal a reduction in Massachusetts in armed robberies and assaults with a gun; the reduction is attributed to the deterrent effect of the new law.[14] No decline is found for homicides, a finding credited to the possibility that, while other criminals are inclined to calculate the costs and benefits of a crime committed with a gun, many homicides occur in the home, typically in the heat of a domestic dispute. Thus, the deterrent effects of the new law on the homicide rate are limited.[15]

Other analyses report even less success in the use of mandatory sentences to deter crimes with a gun. The 1975 Florida felony firearm law mandates a three-year sentence for firearm possession when committing or attempting any of eleven felonies. "The simplest interpretation of the data is that the Florida gun law did not have a measurable deterrent effect on violent crime."[16] This analysis supports a previous study that finds no deterrent effects for a similar mandatory sentencing law in Detroit.[17]

If one takes the argument of deterrence theory to its ultimate, it might be supposed that the most violent crimes can best be deterred by the most severe punishment. Thus, it is not surprising that capital punishment has entered the deterrence literature, especially since executions in the United States resumed in 1977. Not unexpectedly, the literature is divided on the effectiveness of this penalty. A consistent and significant relation was found between frequency of execution and number of homicides per capita.[18] In addition, a relation was discovered between number of arrests, frequency of conviction, and number of homicides. Research in Canada and Great Britain supports the American findings.[19] "Even potential murderers appear to obey the law of demand."[20]

If one takes the sheer number of articles and books that oppose the deterrence hypothesis for capital punishment, the weight of the evidence is against deterrence.[21] An analysis of murders in Chicago challenges the deterrence hypothesis directly.[22] Its major thesis is that capital punishment may encourage killings by promoting a climate of violence. As a remedy, social scientists, rather than relying on the number or rate of homicides, must develop "independent indicators of deterrent and brutalization effects of executions" and attempt "to identify sub-segments of the population that are differentially affected by executions due to deterrence and brutalization, and then examine their differential involvement in murder."[23] The net effect of the mix of deterrence and brutalization, it is argued, is to increase homicides. These variables need to be developed conceptually, which may be difficult, considering that aggregate-level data are employed. Earlier studies disaggregated first- and second-degree murder (with the thesis that deterrence is more effective in the former case) and found that the average homicide rate for either offense was higher in death penalty states than in those that had abolished capital punishment.[24]

Antideterrence effects are also found in a cross-national study that compares homicide rates before and after the abolition of capital punishment in several Western nations.[25] The study demonstrates that the homicide rate tends to decline after the death penalty is terminated. Another study examines the relation between four recent executions in the United States (beginning with Gary Gilmor).[26] Using interrupted time-series analysis, the study finds no correlation between the executions and the homicide rate. In addition, an examination in the state of execution and in surrounding states finds no local effects.

The literature on capital punishment as a deterrent can be criticized on two grounds: the specification of the dependent variable, and the difficulty of ascertaining the motives of individuals from the aggregate data. On the specification problem, many of the capital punishment studies, especially less recent ones, do not distinguish homicides that might result from passion or domestic instability from those that are a product of rational calculation by the murderer. This failure would seem to make the deterrent effect of capital punishment dubious for those who commit murder, other than murder in the first degree, who are probably unlikely deterred by the threat of execution. On the second criticism, it is improbable that dividing homicides into first and second degree can classify individuals' motives other than in a simplistic manner. However, the same may be said about a variety of social behaviors (including drinking and driving), which are difficult if not impossible to measure at the individual level.

In summary, the evidence that punishment, severe or otherwise, deters crime is mixed at best. An even weaker picture emerges when the field of traffic violations is examined.

## *DETERRENCE AND TRAFFIC SAFETY*

As in other areas of criminal justice, most experiments (quasi-experiments may be the more accurate term) in law reform and traffic safety hold deterrence as the central theory in reducing injury and death on the highway. Traditionally, attempts to standardize and enforce penalties for drinking and driving produce either no effect on casualties or simply a short-term impact.[27] Two factors have been cited as contributing heavily to the ineffectiveness of drinking and driving laws. First, usually after a short start-up period, drivers begin to perceive the low probability of apprehension. Second, unlike more conventional types of crimes, the drinking and driving offense is committed frequently and is woven into the social fabric of many modern cultures.[28] As a result, police and judges can have difficulty in enforcing the law consistently and in punishing offenders.

The earliest attempts to impact the drinking and driving problem took place in Scandinavia.[29] Two laws were passed: a 1936 law in Norway and one similar in content in Sweden in 1941. In contrast to the classic approach to drinking and driving, which consists of police observing clinical symptoms of drunkenness, the Scandinavian laws specify blood-alcohol concentrations for use by the police. The Norwegian law sets a minimum of 50 milligrams of alcohol per 1,000 milliliters of blood, or 0.05 percent. The Swedish law sets two levels of violation, one for a concentration of 150 milligrams of alcohol and over and a lesser infraction of 80–149 milligrams; the minimum concentration is now 50 milligrams.

The Scandinavian laws were developed during a time when the technology for ascertaining alcohol-related crimes was improving, especially with the introduction of the breathalyzer. In addition, punishments for the offenses were severe. Driver's license suspension and imprisonment were applied to offenders routinely, especially at higher blood-alcohol concentration levels. In addition, punishment was prompt. But despite the improved technology and the severity of the laws, whether they were effective is open to debate. The difficulty of clearly establishing the effectiveness of these laws rests with two factors: the limitations of available data and the social conditions of the Scandinavian nations at this time.

With regard to the data, only yearly observations of fatalities were analyzed.[30] More sensitive measures, such as night and weekend series contrasted against data gathered during the day as well as against monthly observations, may have produced more valid and reliable conclusions. "Other historical circumstances" may account for fatal crashes, especially in the years immediately following passage.[31] Such factors include poor road conditions and an unsophisticated driving population. (The lower quality of automobiles should be added.) Also, these countries already had severe penalties for drinking and driving, and little publicity appears to have occurred around the time of passage of the laws. Thus, the laws may not have had the shock value in Scandinavia that they had in other Western nations. The deterrent effect of the laws (however small) might be attributable primarily to "habit formation and moral education," such as general support for the laws and a low proportion of drinking drivers on the highways.[32] To a great extent, Scandinavia is an atypical case, because of widespread popular support for temperance.[33]

While other adaptations of the Scandinavian style laws

have taken place (in the Netherlands, Canada, and New Zealand, among others), the most publicized in the scholarly literature have occurred in Britain and France. Both nations typify the application of the Scandinavian approach, in that deterrent effects were found only in the short run.

The Scandinavian approach as applied to Great Britain was manifested under the provisions of the British Road Safety Act of 1967.[34] Before 1967, the approach to apprehending drinking drivers was "modified classical legislation," under which blood tests were used and considered in combination with police observation of the driver's condition.[35] No minimum blood-alcohol concentration was set to define a violation. The 1967 act set a minimum blood-alcohol concentration of 0.08 (80 milligrams of alcohol to 100 milliliters of blood) to define the violation. While the use of roadblocks was eliminated from the proposed legislation because of public and commercial objection, police could apply the breathalyzer in the case of an accident, a moving violation, or a suspicion that a driver had been drinking. (The latter condition is analogous to the concept of probable cause in the United States.) While loopholes in the act were never closed fully, the law was well publicized and penalties for its violation were stiff. Under its terms, a one year suspension of the driver's license was possible.

The British breathalyzer experiment not only is a landmark in innovative legislation to combat drinking and driving, but also is associated with a striking improvement in the use of social science in the analysis of policy problems in general and traffic safety in particular. By using interrupted time-series analysis, Laurence Ross was successful in developing and testing more sensitive measures of alcohol-related crashes. He examined casualties before and after the law was in place and was able to isolate fatalities and serious injuries for weekend nights, a time period when drinking and driving is most likely to occur. He compared these observations to a control series, which included morning and evening commuting hours when pubs were closed. A dramatic reduction in casualties was found immediately following the law's effective date in the weekend night series, a reduction absent from the daytime observations.

The use of the control series enabled Ross to rule out rival hypotheses and helped him establish the law's efficacy more firmly. Unfortunately, the effects were not permanent. An all-time low was reached in October 1967, the effective month of the legislation, but fatalities and injuries inched upward through the following months and years. Ross attributes the temporary effects to the fact that after a short period of alarm, which reduced drinking and driving, the public began to perceive—correctly—that the chances of apprehension were low. While enforcement for those arrested was firm, the number of police available for dealing with drinking drivers remained about the same. "The obvious benefits of drinking and driving—inexpensive and convenient transportation in connection with a normal, alcohol-related social life—overwhelmed the deterrent effect of the British Road Safety Act."[36]

A law similar to the British act was put into effect in France in July 1978. The provisions of the French law were similar to the British, with a few notable exceptions. First, a minimum blood alcohol concentration was set at .08; however, the police actually calibrated the breathalyzers at 0.05.[37] Driving with concentrations above this level could result in revocation instead of suspension of the driver's license. Most important, the French law provided that an individual could be stopped at a roadblock and tested without police suspicion that the driver had been drinking or that a violation had occurred. In short, the idea of probable cause, as espoused in American jurisprudence and adopted in the British Road Safety Act, was absent from the French legislation. While public protest of the British Road Safety Act was considerable, opposition to the French legislation probably was greater. The restaurant and beverage industries especially were incensed as was the public at large. The high national wine consumption and the traditional French affinity for individual liberty made this law an especially unpopular one.

An analysis of the effectiveness of this law used methodology similar to the British case and found near identical results.[38] Fatal and serious crashes and weekend night crashes all dropped temporarily. The findings are stronger for the northern French provinces, where wine production and drinking is heavier. As in Britain, the change in behavior of the French public was not permanent, and fatal and serious crashes returned to normal levels. Again, the law's failure to achieve permanent reductions is attributed to the low probability of apprehension. Perhaps it is especially difficult to regulate drinking and driving in a nation where alcohol is well integrated into normal social dining patterns. Similar laws have been passed and evaluated in the Netherlands, Canada, Australia, and New Zealand, with results similar to those observed in France and Great Britain.[39]

### *Severity of Punishment*

One criticism of drinking-driving laws is that penalties are not severe enough to cause citizens to alter their behavior. Accordingly, it has been argued that penalties must be harsher in order to deter drinking and driving. In many of the recent state laws enacted in the United States, the idea of severity is an important component. However, the literature reveals that increasing penalties to deter drunken driving does little to alter the pattern of fatalities and injuries. Moreover, the judicial system seems reluctant to enforce the law. For example, the 1950 Finnish law that doubled the maximum penalty for drinking and driving did not result in increased sentences.[40] Subsequent analysis demonstrates that the use of prison sentences throughout Scandinavia has declined, without increasing the number of drinking drivers on the highway.[41]

One of the earliest attempts at severe punishment in the United States occurred in Washington State, in Yakima County.[42] The Task Force on Drinking and Driving drafted judicial guidelines, which recommended a two-day jail sentence for driving while intoxicated (DWI). A chief problem of the guidelines is that, while they were "ostensibly mandatory," it was a "recommended" policy to be used at the discretion of the courts. While the policy had a positive impact on the attitudes of the police and the public, it had virtually no effect on alcohol involvement in fatal crashes, even though Yakima County had a rate lower than the rest of the state. The lack of impact is attributed to low public awareness (even though an extensive publicity campaign took place), low probability of arrest, and inconsistency in judicial enforcement.

Similar problems were apparent in California, where a January 1982 law contained a provision for a two-day jail sentence for first offenders.[43] Fatalities did not decrease during the first nine months following passage of the law.[44] Subsequent analysis indicates a lack of a deterrent effect in fatalities during the first year of the law; however, a significant downward impact was achieved for injuries.[45] Incidents of alcohol-impaired driving declined during the law's second year of enforcement, although it is more difficult to attribute the reduction exclusively to the law. On the other hand, there was an increase in the number of jury trials for those accused, a 10 percent decrease in convictions, and a 10.5 percent decrease in guilty pleas.[46] In addition, judges were reluctant to impose the jail sentence. Perhaps the most prominent violator was entertainer Johnny Carson, who received a heavy fine and probation in lieu of a jail sentence in 1983.

In Tennessee, a study funded by the National Highway Traffic Safety Administration (NHTSA) documents difficulties with Tennessee's 1982 law that mandates a two-day jail sentence for first-time DUI offenders. In terms of general deterrence, the research team finds no evidence of a decline in alcohol-related crashes. They recommend more experimentation with the mandatory jail law but believe it would continue to be ineffective without a large amount of publicity. In addition, problems with the handling of DUI cases by the criminal justice system were similar to California's. In summarizing their findings, the NHTSA researchers advise "states considering adopting a tough mandatory jail law to be both skeptical and extremely cautious."[47] Thus, the analysis of several state laws confirm the results in Scandinavia—there is lack of consistent impact on casualties, and dislocations occur in the administration, enforcement, and sentencing under the law.

One example of where a jail sentence appears to have worked is in Hennepin County (Minneapolis), Minnesota, where nighttime accidents involving injuries declined within two months after judges adopted a policy of sentencing all first-time alcohol-related offenders to serve two days in jail.[48] The policy was facilitated because in this area of Minnesota jails were not overcrowded, as they were in other parts of the nation. Difficulties reported in other states regarding dislocations in the criminal justice system were minimal. Also, the policy received wide publicity and was supported by the public.

### *Swift and Sure Punishment*

As in the criminal justice literature cited earlier, the lack of a relation between severity and deterrence led social scientists concerned with drinking and driving to explore other avenues to change behavior. For example, there have been experiments with increasing the certainty and swiftness of punishment. Major criticisms made by groups such as Mothers Against Drunk Driving (MADD) are that not only are existing laws and judges too lenient in dealing with the problem, but also an offender often is able to manipulate the legal system to both delay and circumvent punishment. Regarding the certainty of punishment, a key variable is the low probability of apprehension. While most drinking and driving laws are successful in the short run, an important element in their long-term failure is that citizens begin to perceive, correctly, that they are unlikely to get caught. Drinking and driving is viewed by many as being necessary and positive for their social or business lives and is a risk they are willing to take. Where attempts have been made to increase enforcement and, hence, the certainty of apprehension (in parts of England, New Zealand, and the United States), results are more in line with a deterrence approach. However, when the threat is removed, established patterns in terms of injuries and deaths tend to return.

Perhaps the most prominent case of increasing the likelihood of detection and punishment of the drinking driver took place in Cheshire, England, where the chief constable, cognizant of the weakening of the 1967 Road Safety Act, began to administer the breathalyzer intensively and randomly during late night hours.[49] Breath testing in Cheshire gradually rose to six times the national average by September 1975. The constable gathered data for the late night hours but also selected a control period between 2 P.M. and 5 P.M. when one might not expect any reduction in injuries and fatalities. The county experienced a drop in road casualties during the period of intense enforcement, which was not evident during the control hours. Because of vehement protests by civil libertarians and automobile clubs, who viewed the experiment as a random test in violation of the law, the "Cheshire blitz" was terminated.

A similar and more recent program in Stockton, California, also achieved success during periods of increased police enforcement.[50] Specifically, ten patrol cars operated by specially trained police officers were added to regular patrols during Friday and Saturday nights between 8 P.M. and 4 A.M. During the program (1976–1979), there were no alterations in the California laws on drinking and driving. Results indicate an accident reduction of approximately 15 percent on weekend nights. A smaller reduction was in evidence on weekday nights during the same period. Also, there was a 20 percent reduction in blood-alcohol concentrations for drivers in Stockton during the project period. Finally, nighttime accidents failed to decline in control cities in the aggregate. The only city with a decline similar to Stockton was Bakersfield, which increased DWI arrests during this time. Overall, Stockton, like Cheshire, suggests that it is probably necessary to raise the certainty of apprehension if more severe penalties are to be effective.

As for swiftness of punishment, several efforts have been made to evaluate the effectiveness of administrative driver's license suspension as an alternative to increasing criminal penalties for drinking and driving.[51] Such laws involve the immediate suspension and confiscation of a driver's license by the police for a driver refusing to take a breathalyzer test or failing it. While a hearing may be held following the suspension, the license rarely is returned.[52]

Administrative license suspension was introduced first in Minnesota in 1976 and slowly spread to seventeen other states. The Minnesota law shows no deterrence effect, and a decline in fatalities is more a manifestation of trends established in the late 1960s.[53] However, administrative license revocation in New Mexico shows more promise of the deterrent effect of increasing the swiftness of punishment.[54] The purpose of the law, which was implemented in July 1984, was to shorten the time between receipt of the citation for driving while intoxicated and paying the penalty. Results are conflicting; many members of the judiciary find the law confusing, and the public has only limited understanding of its provisions. Despite these facts, for the first twenty months following implementation, there was a significant drop in vehicle and pedestrian alcohol-related fatalities. Moreover, this reduction seems permanent.[55]

Another strategy that eliminates some of the complexities of administrative license suspension is mandatory license suspension, which operates in Wisconsin and Michigan.[56] In Wisconsin, a law effective in May 1982 mandates three- to six-month license suspension for first-time offenders. Nighttime accidents involving injury and single vehicles with a male driver were significantly reduced, and recidivism dropped.[57] Thus the Wisconsin law had a convincing deterrent effect, which up to this time was absent in studies both of European nations and of other American states.

## *THE CONCEPT OF GENERAL PREVENTION*

In examining laws designed to deter drinking and driving, a number of social scientists assert that while interrupted time-series analysis is a valid method of detecting legal effects in the short term, it is more questionable in examining changes in casualties in the long run.[58] The limitations of the time-series technique are illustrated by the Scandinavian experience, which cannot be explained adequately by changes in behavior in response to law.[59] Rather, the low incidence of drinking and driving in Norway and Sweden can be understood more completely by taking into account a complex array of sociological and contextual factors. Among these variables are psychological ones; Scandinavians perceive the drinking and driving offense as a much more severe crime than do Americans. Similarly, social controls, at least until recently, were more lax in the United States, as evidenced by the casual enforcement of drinking and driving laws. Other important factors in Scandinavia include a temperance movement tradition, strict control over the supply of alcoholic beverages (including a high tax rate), availability of public transportation, consistent enforcement of penalties, and, above all, strong support by the public for enforcement and punishment under the law.[60] These contextual factors are forceful deterrents and have an impact equal to or greater than legislation.[61]

In contrast, the United States does not have a tradition of intolerance of drinking and driving nor strong federal policies on the control or distribution of alcohol. Instead, states direct these policies, with wide variations. Still, a number of developments occurred in the 1980s that might be classified as general prevention by the federal government. Included in these measures are changes in the legal drinking age and mandatory seat belt use. These laws are not primarily deterrents, because in the case of many drinking-age laws, penalties for violation are usually placed on suppliers rather than consumers. For seat belt laws, penalties are minimal and enforcement provisions often weak. While other aspects of general prevention are harder to measure—such as an emphasis on healthful life style and physical fitness—drinking-age laws and mandatory seat belt use can be incorporated into an interrupted time-series design and may help explain changes in casualties in the long term, apart from the initial effects of a reform in drinking and driving laws. Like laws regarding drinking and driving, these laws have become important options for policy makers interested in lowering the casualty rate on the highways. A considerable body of literature has been amassed on these more generally preventive laws in recent years, much of it favorable to public safety.

### *Drinking-Age Laws*

Because of concern about the abuse of alcohol by many young persons and its consequence on the highway, raising the legal drinking age has been used as a major policy instrument.[62]

While it is widely realized that raising the drinking age will not completely prohibit people from obtaining alcohol, it will at least make availability, and hence consumption, more difficult. In addition, raising the drinking age is likely to make access especially troublesome for the very young driver. For example, in a state that raises the drinking age from eighteen to twenty-one, one would imagine that access would become many times more difficult for sixteen- and seventeen-year-olds.[63]

The majority of the literature on the minimum legal drinking age and its relation to injuries and fatalities supports the proposition that these laws tend to reduce casualties significantly. Maine and Michigan, which raised the drinking age in the late 1970s, were compared to two control states, New York and Pennsylvania, which left the drinking age unchanged for the period of study.[64] Using interrupted time series, the study finds reductions in property damage accidents related to alcohol in the experimental states, while similar results are not found in the control states. In addition, declines are apparent among the young affected by the new laws and are not evident in older drivers. The reduction in accidents not related to alcohol is far smaller than the reduction in alcohol-related crashes, and this decline in alcohol-related crashes cannot be attributed to any change in alcohol sales.

This outcome seems consistent with earlier research on lowering the drinking age in Michigan (to age eighteen in 1972). That work confirms the effects of a lower drinking age on property damage and injury-producing crashes. While the study demonstrates an approximate 20 percent drop in serious crashes, another study indicates a 17 percent *increase* following a lowering of the drinking age.[65] Finally, while the first study analyzes data for the six months following the passage of the December 1978 law in Michigan, additional research analyzes the effect of the law through 1984.[66] While Wagenaar could find no significant decline in single-vehicle, nighttime crashes for those under age twenty-one, those twenty-one and over experienced a 17 percent *increase* in such accidents. In the long term, the law may have prevented those age eighteen through twenty from a similar upward trend.

While the literature generally hypothesizes that an increase in the drinking age has its greatest effect after an abrupt drinking-age change from age eighteen to twenty-one, reductions in casualties also resulted from a 1981 Texas law that raised the drinking age to nineteen.[67] Specifically, there was a decline in single-vehicle, nighttime crashes for eighteen-year-olds for all categories of crash severity. Similar findings were not evident for those twenty-one and over. Macroeconomic conditions did not affect crash involvement (as measured by an industrial production index).

A comprehensive study published in 1983 by the Insurance Institute for Highway Safety examines the effects of changes in the drinking age in nine states and contrasts the results with data from neighboring states that did not raise the drinking age.[68] The study demonstrates an average reduction of 28 percent in fatal nighttime crashes in eight of the nine states. A similar reduction is not evident in the control states. The institute study challenges a study using data from the Fatal Accident Reporting System, where a seesaw effect was observed.[69] "Nighttime fatal crashes involving drivers of the old drinking age are reduced, while nighttime fatal crashes involving drivers of the new drinking age increase in roughly the same proportion."[70] While the latter study has been challenged for its methodology,[71] it raises the possibility that the key variable may not be drinking age itself but inexperience with drinking.

The hypothesis that inexperience with drinking rather than the minimum legal age is a primary variable in youthful traffic fatalities was investigated through the use of cross-sectional data.[72] The dependent variable was total fatalities, single-vehicle fatalities, and single-vehicle, nighttime fatalities. The results indicate no relation between the drinking age and fatalities; in contrast, inexperience in drinking (as measured by whether or not a cohort was of drinking age), demonstrates a strong and significant relation to the fatality rate. Moreover, results are insensitive to which fatality rate was used. This led the authors to conclude that a legal drinking age is of limited policy usefulness. Rather, what is needed for those at the minimum age is education about alcohol and its risks. Further, there may be some benefits to introducing young persons gradually to alcohol use. As it currently exists, the legal minimum age could be too abrupt a change in some people's lives, causing social disfunctions for society at large.

The fact that a change in the drinking age cannot account completely for reductions in youthful fatalities has led to the exploration of other policy options.[73] Inexperience with drinking is an acknowledged factor in the high casualty rate of youth on the highway, but another important variable is the short time young people have been driving. Inexperience on the road can be as dangerous as inexperience with alcohol. Accordingly, a number of policy options have been explored, including raising the age when one may obtain a license to drive and limiting the hours of vehicle operation (eliminating night hours).[74] In general, enforcing laws that limit the hours driven or raising the age to qualify for a driver's license may lower the rate of casualties and fatalities in many localities.[75]

While it is beyond the scope of this study to discuss and evaluate all of these alternatives, it should be kept in mind that the drinking age is only one of several policy options available and, when used alone, may not be sufficient to lessen the dangers of driving by the young. The impact of these laws may be especially limited when one considers that youths (especially males) are more likely than the remainder of the population to drink and drive and are less likely to employ the third intervention considered in this study—the seat belt.[76]

### *Seat Belt Laws*

The seat belt and laws mandating its use is a second policy option under the heading of general prevention. Adopted earlier in Europe, mandatory use laws have been implemented in the United States during the 1980s, along with alcohol-impaired driving and minimum drinking age legislation, to lessen traffic casualties. The overall effectiveness of the mandatory use of seat belts has been established in terms of fatality reduction.[77] However, achieving compliance is a problem, especially in the United States and Canada. Where compliance is high, as in Great Britain, results are impressive.

In general, compliance is higher outside of the United States.[78] For example, my study of highway casualties in England and Wales after the passage of the 1983 law hypothesizes that the drop in casualties would be temporary.[79] This reasoning was based on the "gradual erosion scenario."[80] The scenario holds that a policy is most likely to achieve compliance in its very early stages when public enthusiasm is high and the bureaucrats who formulated the policy supervise its implementation. As the issue loses focus and impetus and administrators move to new positions, policy enforcement declines, as does public support. In addition, previous research on the Canadian experience suggests that compliance was high immediately after the passage of seat belt legislation (around 70 percent) but declined with time (the long-term compliance rate was about 50 percent).[81]

Given that the fine was fifty pounds in Britain with no penalty points on the driver's license, it was hypothesized that compliance would be high at first but would gradually erode. With lower compliance, fatalities and injuries would again rise. But compliance turned out higher than anyone imagined, exceeding 95 percent by the second year. As a consequence, a seemingly permanent reduction in fatalities and serious injuries was demonstrated through the second year of implementation. The high compliance in Britain may be due to that nation's comparatively long history of supporting traffic safety interventions.[82] However, the reason for such responsibility in comparison to Canada and the United States is not altogether clear.

Even though compliance is much lower in the United States, a considerable body of work demonstrates that use of seat belts lessens the casualty rate on the highway. For example, a study using a Poisson statistical model of the first U.S. state to pass a mandatory law (New York) estimates that during the first six months of enforcement 220 fatalities, 1,500 severe injuries, 4,600 moderate injuries, and 2,600 light injuries were averted because of the law.[83] A subsequent analysis indicates more modest results—a fatality reduction of 9 percent in the first nine months of the law.[84] Still, the results seem impressive, as compliance with the law approximated only 57 percent at its peak.

Positive results are also to be found in other states, but the results are uneven. Much depends on the nature of the law and the enforcement level. A comprehensive study of the first eight states with mandatory seat belt laws reveals a significant reduction of 8.7 percent in front seat fatalities following the passage of these laws, a decline generally greater than in comparison states.[85] Reductions in back seat and nonoccupant fatalities were evident. Interestingly, fatality reduction was stronger in states with primary enforcement than in those with secondary enforcement (9.9 percent to 6.7 percent). Primary enforcement allows investigation for only violation of the seat belt law; secondary enforcement allows investigation only when another law has been broken. Still, the decline among secondary-enforcement states was statistically significant.

The study is supported by work from the University of North Carolina Highway Safety Research Center, which examined seat belt laws in twenty-four states and the District of Columbia.[86] Fatalities through December 1986 were examined, using a forecasting technique. A 6.6 percent reduction in fatalities over what was predicted if the laws had not taken effect was found. This amounts to 1,300 fewer fatalities in these states. In states not covered by such laws, there was no improvement.[87]

Lack of compliance with seat belt laws presents a difficult problem, because most often those who refuse to comply are among the highest risk drivers.[88] Following the passage of the seat belt law in New York State, teenagers had a lower rate of seat belt use than the population at large, and males were less likely to comply than females.[89] Further, high-speed drivers, even though they improved their seat belt use considerably, had the lowest rates of seat belt use.[90] Fast drivers also tend to have more prior violations than slow-speed drivers, greatly increasing their crash risk. Attitude toward seat belt use correlates with other aspects of a healthful life style. For example, heavy smokers who do not wear seat belts are more likely to drive after drinking.[91]

Because compliance is crucial to the ultimate success of seat belt laws, a variety of strategies have been attempted to encourage use. A review of the impact of twenty-eight incentive programs in nine work settings finds that compliance increased from 12 percent to 285 percent over baseline use.[92] Although compliance dropped after program termination, postprogram levels only rarely declined to the usage rate for the period before the program was implemented. Interestingly, the lasting impact was greatest in those programs that involve no extrinsic rewards.

Prior to the passage of a seat belt law in North Carolina, a communitywide incentive program was implemented in the Chapel Hill area. The incentive program consisted of opportunities to win cash and other prizes donated by local businesses and to participate in drawings worth up to $1,000. Shoulder belt use was monitored at different phases of the program. At its peak, the area achieved a usage rate of 41 percent which at the time was equal to the highest recorded in any U.S. community.[93]

While incentive programs have been successful, they have been criticized as weak and inconsistent in the development of program theory.[94] A second approach to increasing compliance is stronger law enforcement combined with publicity. An experiment in British Columbia indicates that citizens may be deterred from driving without using a seat belt if the certainty of apprehension is increased.[95] In that province, compliance jumped from 33 to 72 percent for front seat drivers immediately following passage of the law in November 1977 but declined to 52 percent by March 1981. The basic aim of the experiment was to increase compliance by increasing the certainty but not the severity of punishment. One community was selected for an intensive media campaign along with increased enforcement, while a second, similar village was used as a control. In the experimental community, the media campaign stressed not only the law's existence but also the probability of a fine for violation. The results of the study demonstrate increased belt use in the test community. Before the experiment, seat belt use stood at 44.6 percent; by the final phase of the project, it rose to 74.4 percent. The highest compliance was achieved for those sixty-five years of age and older. This group was approximately 20 percentage points higher than their younger cohorts. Similar behavior did not occur among motorists in the control group. The study concludes that legal sanctions can have a deterrent effect if certainty of punishment is increased and if citizens are made aware of the consequences of violation.

On a national level, government publicity programs have been successful in Canada and the Netherlands. For example, in the Canadian provinces, seat belt use achieved a high of approximately 70 percent at the inception of the law but declined to close to 50 percent with the passage of time.[96] Through Canada's selective traffic enforcement programs (STEP), compliance has increased drastically.[97] The STEP program involves a two-week prior notice of primary enforcement, followed by intensive publicity in the media and through mailings and public presentations. Simultaneously, there are checks for seat belt use and more citations are issued. Results among the provinces have been highly successful, with British Columbia climbing from 58 to 73 percent. The highest province was Quebec (86 percent) and even low-use provinces such as Prince Edward Island, Manitoba, Newfoundland, and New Brunswick exceeded use in most U.S. states where mandatory use laws are in effect. Presumably, higher compliance ultimately will lead to fewer injuries and fatalities on the highways. As the most recent findings show that compliance is a severe problem in the United States, even in states with mandatory use laws, more work must be undertaken to address this issue.[98]

## *THEORETICAL FRAMEWORK*

A review of criminal justice literature in general and traffic safety policy literature in particular documents the limitations of the deterrence approach to moderating human behavior. Drinking and driving is especially troublesome because those in law enforcement and the judiciary do not view such traffic violations as conventional crimes.[99]

Deterrence can be viewed as a legal attempt to change custom.[100] The success of such an attempt is dependent upon the following factors:

- the utilitarian and moral significance of the custom to its adherents;
- the popular support a custom enjoys;
- the visibility of the custom to law enforcement agencies;
- whether the custom is of such a nature that a general change may extinguish individual drives to follow it; and

- whether a change in the custom meets current community needs.[101]

Drinking and driving and underage drinking have high value for its participants in most modern societies. For example, in many U.S. cities, especially in growing sunbelt areas, extensive freeway systems coupled with poor public transportation in the late hours, and bars, discos, and nightclubs located in outlying areas, combine to encourage drinking and driving. Such a situation exists in cities such as Los Angeles, Atlanta, and Phoenix. For many who place social interaction high on their personal agenda, social drinking is apparently of high priority and the automobile the most convenient method of transportation. The benefits to them of drinking and driving thus outweigh the low risk of apprehension and punishment.

While severity of punishment for the underage drinker also is high in some states, risk of apprehension probably is low and penalties are most frequently placed on the supplier of the alcohol. Much of the risk of apprehension may depend on whether the underage drinker drinks on public premises, where the threat of arrest is more likely than if the alcohol is consumed in the home or at private parties. In either case, for many young people, especially those over age eighteen, considerable importance is placed on social situations involving alcohol. The benefits are perhaps perceived to be greater than the risks involved in being caught.

The reason that so many citizens refuse to wear seat belts does not seem to be explained by the utility/morality proposition. Lack of compliance may be explained best by either a dearth of information about the benefits of seat belts or the low risk of apprehension and the relatively small penalties assessed for not wearing the belt.[102] Because the seat belt is morally neutral, it may fail to generate the normative dilemma posed by the other two interventions. So in changing citizens' behavior, government may have more success with the seat belt.

In terms of popularity, the extensive publicity on drinking and driving and the dangerous aspects of youth involvement in alcohol and drugs have made such activities less culturally acceptable to society as a whole. An important factor in instilling these negative perceptions is the success that government and society have had in establishing a link between improper use of alcohol and negative health consequences. Less success has been achieved in making the public aware of the dangers of noncompliance with mandatory seat belt use. In addition, the public seems less willing to accept scientific evidence on their effectiveness. Political leadership is divided as well. While American and British politicians could not possibly go on record as being opposed to drunk-driving laws, many have publicly viewed the seat belt as either ineffective or an infringement on individual liberties.[103] So in terms of legislation, stricter drinking and driving laws and underage drinking laws may be more popular than seat belt laws. Nevertheless, while many citizens support drunk-driving legislation, they do not always comply with the laws.

The probability of apprehension for all traffic safety violations is low. For drunken driving, one estimate claims that a driver would have to commit between 200 and 2,000 violations in order to be apprehended.[104] Enforcement would have to increase many times over (perhaps a score) in order to pose an effective risk to the violator. Chances of apprehension are even smaller for those violating the minimum drinking-age and seat belt laws. In the case of the seat belt, roadside surveys of compliance show a high level of violation and a comparatively low level of penalty in the form of citations. Typically, compliance among the states is at 50 percent and under, even in states with primary enforcement. While checking for noncompliance is relatively easy, government has not devoted the energy to enforcing seat belt laws as it has drinking and driving laws. For the underage drinker, chances of apprehension are slim, unless that violation is combined with a driving offense. While underage drinking may raise highway fatalities and injuries, consumption also takes place without any vehicle involvement. Consequently, enforcement of the law will have only a limited effect on highway casualties.

In addition to the apprehension problem, the likelihood of severe punishment actually being imposed is low. This applies especially to laws governing drinking and driving. In instances where penalties are especially severe, as in cases of mandatory sentencing, the literature demonstrates a reluctance by the judiciary to impose the punishment.[105] Much of the difficulty in enforcement and punishment in the case of seat belts, the minimum drinking age, and the drinking driver is related to the violator's social characteristics: specifically, "the general relationship between success in suppressing a custom and perceived likelihood of apprehension is that broader law enforcement means arresting greater numbers of high status people for violation."[106]

There is some evidence that the situation is beginning to change, especially in the United States. The 1980s witnessed the passage of legislation against drinking and driving in nearly every U.S. state. Not only does this legislation raise and standardize the penalties for drinking and driving, but also it increases the certainty and swiftness of punishment. Also, the legislation is often coupled with vigorous enforcement campaigns. If drinking and driving laws are combined with preventive strategies, such as seat belt laws, drinking-age laws, and supportive public attitudes, one might expect more impressive results than are possible under simple deterrence. For example, an Insurance Institute for Highway Safety study examines fatal crashes in states with, among them, three types of laws against alcohol-impaired driving, including mandatory jail sentences, administrative license suspension and per se laws (which define a maximum permissible blood alcohol concentration).[107] Overall, the study finds that in 1985 approximately 1,560 drivers avoided fatal accidents due to these laws.

Most American communities have recently been saturated by accounts of the tragedies created by poor safety practices on highways. Consideration of changing usual highway customs is the result. Current community behavior is being challenged because of death and injury on the highway and because of the emotional and physical suffering and financial loss generated by this behavior. This book examines the effects of a few of the more innovative new laws in three U.S. states and in Great Britain. While severity of punishment varies, the new laws are usually coupled with a greater certainty of apprehension and provide fewer options for the offender, once caught. Also, we examine both the deterrent aspects of the laws and their preventive strategies, like raising the minimum legal drinking age and requiring the use of seat belts.

## *HYPOTHESES*

When the drinking and driving problem is set into the theoretical framework of deterrence, there would seem little hope that government interventions have a great effect on the problem. In contrast, the Insurance Institute for Highway Safety study suggests that more recent laws have been fruitful, at least in the United States. Also, the general environment of prevention as promoted by groups such as Mothers Against Drunk Driving (MADD) and Students Against Driving Drunk (SADD) coupled with more awareness in recent years on the dangers of abusing alcohol may have helped reduce casualties more permanently following the passage of legislation.

Still, with regard to drinking and driving laws in New York, California, and Michigan, I choose the more conservative hypothesis. Specifically, in line with much of the traditional literature on drinking and driving, I hypothesize a short-term effect on fatalities. While the more consistent and certain penalties may lessen casualties significantly, some evidence suggests that in a few of the states, the new laws have had no deterrent impact.[108]

> *Hypothesis 1*: Laws that impose stricter penalties for drinking and driving will reduce fatalities in the first few months following their implementation but will have no deterrent effect over the long run.

The literature is divided on the question of changing the drinking age, and it is difficult to formulate a hypothesis confidently. While short- and long-term reductions in casualtics have been documented in Michigan and other states, some contend that the age at which casualties occur has merely risen, and overall rates of injury and death have not changed. While the weight of the evidence is probably on the side of a higher minimum drinking age, there is a temptation to state the hypothesis in null terms because of these ambiguities in the literature. However, since the effects of policy should be judged in connection with the intent of the policy maker,[109] I base hypothesis 2 on the policy maker's intent—that an increase in the drinking age will reduce traffic fatalities.

> *Hypothesis 2*: Laws that raise the minimum legal drinking age will reduce fatalities over both the short and long term. The reduction will be greatest for those directly addressed by the laws.

Finally, a number of studies demonstrate that seat belts are effective in reducing fatalities, although in the United States, long-range evidence is largely absent, given the relative newness of many of these laws. Still, a key issue is compliance. We might expect such laws to be effective only in jurisdictions with primary enforcement and continuous compliance. While high compliance is difficult to achieve, recent evidence from Canada, the Netherlands, and the United States suggests that publicity coupled with increased enforcement can elevate seat belt use considerably.[110]

> *Hypothesis 3*: Laws mandating seat belt use will reduce highway fatalities. However, the effect will be conditional: if compliance is high, the reduction will be long-term; if compliance is low, the reduction will be short-term.

The methodology for testing the hypotheses is presented in chapter 3.

# 3

## *RESEARCH DESIGN AND METHODOLOGY*

*

*THE BASIC RESEARCH* design usually used in analyzing policy interventions is one or more variations of the simple interrupted time-series design. The use of time-series analysis is especially prevalent in the traffic safety literature. The chief advantages of such designs are their control over causal inference and their rigorous statistical methodology, which can eliminate alternative explanations to policy interventions.

### *EXPERIMENTATION AND TIME-SERIES RESEARCH DESIGNS*

In both basic and applied social research, the experimental design holds the greatest potential to confirm a relation between program treatment and outcome.[1] In the experiment, the investigator controls both the treatment, or independent variable, and the subjects. By assigning subjects to treatment and control groups on a random basis, the investigator minimizes the possibility that outcomes are due to systematic differences between the two groups. Because the investigator also controls the independent variable, level of treatment can be manipulated throughout the experiment. In applied social research, however, the situation usually is radically different. For example, in the public arena, investigations of the effects of laws, regulations, and policies take place in a complex of public and private institutions and settings. Typically, the investigator had little or no part in the enactment of these laws and has no control over their implementation.

Because of the lack of control over treatment, subjects, and the circumstances under which treatment is administered, it is often necessary for social scientists to use quasi-experimental research designs. The chief distinguishing characteristic of the quasi-experiment in contrast to the experiment (including those administered in the field) is that the random assignment of subjects to treatment and control groups is not possible. Also, investigators typically cannot manipulate the treatment variable.

One type of quasi-experimental design is the time-series method.[2] Its chief advantage over other types of quasi-experiments is the typically large number of observations before and after treatment, which usually allows a more sophisticated and rigorous analysis. In addition, the use of a control series, where one would not normally expect a change, can often eliminate alternative hypotheses. The chief disadvantage of the time-series design is that, typically, it is viewed retrospectively. In many other quasi-experiments, the researcher may have at least limited control of the treatment variable.

## *TIME-SERIES DESIGNS*

The most elementary of time-series designs is the simple interrupted design. All other designs based on periodic observations are variations on the simple interrupted design. It is diagrammed as follows.

$$O_1\ O_2\ O_3\ X\ O_4\ O_5\ O_6$$

The *X* represents the independent or treatment variable expected to affect the *O*s, which are observations of the dependent variable. The observations must be made at equal intervals, usually on a monthly basis, when traffic safety interventions are considered. It is the task of the research design to detect an effect in the series that is not due to cyclical or random variations, seasonal shifts, or instability.

The simple interrupted design is the weakest of the time-series designs, because of its problems of history and instrumentation.[3] The history problem is illustrated by the possibility that events occurring in the policy environment other than the intervention could be responsible for change in the dependent variable of interest. For example, a state may pass a law designed to reduce driving under the influence of alcohol, and officials subsequently may notice a drop in traffic fatalities. The reduction may well be due to the law itself. Or it may be due to a reduction in the number of miles driven or a decline in the amount of alcohol consumed. Certainly both of the latter alternatives must be explored before one could be completely confident of the effects of the new law. The problem of instrumentation is especially prevalent in time-series designs because of the possibility of an alteration in the definition of a variable at any point in the series or a change in the person recording the information. For example, what might be considered a serious, as opposed to a slight, injury could vary over time.

One strategy used to compensate for the problems of history and instrumentation has been the use of one or more control series. In the traffic safety field, the best known and one of the earliest uses of control series occurred in the analysis of the 1985 Connecticut crackdown on speeding.[4] To punish speeders, new penalties were added, including suspension of driver's licenses. At the end of the first year of the new enforcement campaign, traffic fatalities were reduced by 12.3

percent. Many attributed the falling number of deaths to the new policy, but the change could have been due to any number of alternative explanations, such as a milder winter season in the Northeast. To investigate these hypotheses, researchers examined trends in fatalities in other northeastern states during the same time period. The addition of the several control series undergirded the argument that the crackdown was responsible for the reduction in fatalities. The control series, or multiple time-series, design is diagrammed as follows:[5]

$$\frac{O_1\ O_2\ O_3\ X\ O_4\ O_5\ O_6}{O_1\ O_2\ O_3\quad\ O_4\ O_5\ O_6}$$

As was the case in the Connecticut crackdown, multiple series can be added to strengthen confidence in the analysis.

Although less frequently used, perhaps a more interesting and innovative design uses the nonequivalent dependent variable.[6] In addition to examining a primary dependent variable, where one would expect change to occur, the social scientist also focuses on other dependent variables where one would not expect change. If a change is evident in the nonequivalent dependent variables as well as in the dependent variable of interest, the inference that a particular policy caused the change is weakened. Plausible rival hypotheses that other factors (especially historical ones) are at work must be investigated more thoroughly.

Perhaps the best known example of nonequivalent design in the traffic safety literature is analysis of the 1967 British breathalyzer crackdown.[7] Researchers explored the hypothesis that adoption of the breathalyzer reduced fatalities and serious injuries in Great Britain. Because British pubs have irregular hours of service, the authors were able to compare serious injuries and fatalities during periods when the pubs were open (especially during the night) to those hours when they were closed (primarily during commuting hours). In general, it was expected that the effect of the breathalyzer would be greatest during the hours when pubs were open and weakest when the pubs were closed. Even though the effect of the breathalyzer appeared to be short-lived, the hypothesis was confirmed. Had there been reductions both in the evening and during commuting hours, the drop in fatalities and serious injuries might not have been attributable to the breathalyzer. Rival hypotheses were explored and found unwarranted. The effects on fatalities and serious injuries of an overall reduction in alcohol consumption, intoxicated drivers being more cautious because of the publicity surrounding the breathalyzer, and reduced driving were negligible.

The time-series design with nonequivalent dependent variables is useful when it is difficult to use the multiple time-series design. When using a multiple time-series design, one would look for control series where no interventions have been attempted, so that they may be compared to the treatment series. Few U.S. states or European nations have not attempted reforms of traffic safety that could affect the variables under consideration. For example, in the 1980s, nearly all U.S. states increased penalties for driving under the influence of alcohol. Almost all have experimented with varying the minimum drinking age (California being an important exception). Also, more than half have implemented a mandatory seat belt use law. Thus, nearly every state has had more than one policy reform, making it difficult to consider any as an untreated control. The most practical strategy, then, is the nonequivalent dependent variable design.

## *THE DEPENDENT VARIABLE AND ITS MEASUREMENT*

The primary dependent variable is the traffic fatality. The use of the traffic fatality alone as a dependent variable has come under criticism in the traffic safety literature. In particular, in analyzing the effect of changing the drinking age, it has been argued that monthly fatalities among people age twenty and under simply are too low to permit a confident analysis.[8] If the sole purpose of this study were to investigate the effects of changing the legal drinking age, the low fatalities would present a problem. However, in addition to examining the effects of drinking-age laws, I will examine the impact of drunk-driving laws and seat belt legislation. Also, I wish to account for the impact that these laws have had on entire populations. Monthly traffic fatalities are much higher if the complete population of a political entity is considered, and because the population of the industrial states analyzed is also high, the number of fatalities is not a major methodological problem.

Using the traffic fatality as the dependent variable also helps to achieve another goal of this book—comparability. While considerable differences exist across political units as to what constitutes a serious injury, little disagreement is possible with regard to fatalities. Both the British and U.S. departments of transportation define a fatality occurring within thirty days of an accident to be the result of the accident.[9] Monthly data from January 1977 through December 1986 are available from Great Britain for England and Wales. Comparable measurements from January 1975 through December 1987 are used for U.S. states. Also, time series over an extended period greatly aids the ability of social science to generalize research findings. Citing the paucity of longitudinal data, James Jacobs point out, "The more years for which statistics on alcohol-related driver fatalities can be calculated, the more confidence we can have in the conclusions."[10]

## *RESEARCH DESIGNS*

Research designs were developed for each political unit—England and Wales, New York, California, and Michigan. The basic approach was a time-series design with multiple interventions. In England and Wales, attention focuses on the 1983 seat belt law and the 1983 Christmas Crusade against drinking and driving. The New York analysis centers on its driving while intoxicated and seat belt reforms as well as its two changes in the minimum legal drinking age. Two interventions are analyzed in California: the 1982 driving under the influence reform and the 1986 seat belt law. Finally, Michigan's change in the legal drinking age, its 1983 drinking and driving reform, and the 1985 seat belt law are examined.

In addition to considering the treatment series with multiple interventions, controls were established through nonequivalent dependent variables. To analyze the effect of drinking and driving reforms, fatal nighttime accidents involving single vehicles with male drivers are compared to similar fatal daytime accidents. The comparison is made because nighttime accidents are much more likely to involve alcohol than daytime accidents. While the Fatal Accident Reporting System does contain the police officer's opinion as to whether drinking was involved in the accident, this variable is not used because of its lack of reliability.[11] For the purposes of this study, nighttime accidents occur between 9 P.M. and 6 A.M., while daytime accidents occur at all other times.

With regard to drinking-age laws, I first analyze the impact of these changes on the entire population in combination with the other interventions. Here, I expect very little impact. Next, I compare the law's effect on the intended groups. For these groups, the impact should be much stronger. Since it has been alleged that raising the legal drinking age negatively affects those recently reaching this age, this impact is examined. Also, I examine the impact of mandatory seat belt use on front seat and back seat passengers in the U.S. states and expect the primary effect to be on drivers and front seat passengers.

Three other variables are especially crucial in the analysis: the total number of miles driven, economic conditions, and trends in alcohol consumption. The annual number of miles driven in the United States varies a great deal. In most states, travel increased gradually from the mid-1970s and then dropped during the recession of the early 1980s. As the price of gasoline began to decline during 1985, travel increased greatly. One indicator of travel previously used is the total amount of gasoline consumed, as estimated from highway revenues. The difficulty with using this measure alone is that more fuel-efficient cars have been developed since the mid-1970s, causing a gradual decline in total gasoline consumption. Thus, monthly gasoline use is not likely to measure accurately increases or decreases in travel. I developed an estimated monthly number of miles driven for each state by dividing the number of miles driven for a given year by the amount of highway gasoline consumed. The number of gallons consumed per month were then multiplied by the estimate of miles per gallon in each state to arrive at the number of miles driven per month.[12] While comparable data are not available for England and Wales on a monthly basis, the number of miles driven annually were examined to check the possibility of a rival explanation.

All of the political entities considered have experienced considerable changes in economic fortune over the years examined. For example, in the United States the recession of the early 1980s emerges as a rival to drunk-driving legislation as an explanation for a drop in traffic fatalities. Two hypotheses have been advanced concerning economic conditions. On the one hand, economic recession may lead to psychological depression and increased alcohol use, leading to more alcohol-impaired driving. This proposition is difficult to substantiate with aggregate-level data. A second and more confirmed hypothesis is that recessions are associated with reduced driving, which leads to lower traffic fatalities. Moreover, the business cycle, as measured by the unemployment rate, affects fatalities independent of miles driven.[13] Accordingly, I used monthly unemployment in Great Britain and the individual states to control the effect of economic conditions on fatalities. This helps ensure that any policy impact cannot be due to variations in the economies.

Annual data on alcohol consumption are compiled in Great Britain and quarterly and yearly data are available from the United States. In general, trends are similar across England and Wales and the United States in that consumption of spirits (liquor) has declined while beer and wine drinking has remained the same or has increased slightly. This variable is important: if drinking habits change drastically over a short period, they may rival the policy intervention as an explanation for a drop in traffic fatalities. A decline in deaths may not be owing to citizens not mixing drinking and driving, but to lower alcohol consumption.

## *THE STATISTICAL METHODOLOGY*

A long time series is available for all the political units under consideration. The shortest is for Great Britain, with 120 observations from January 1977 through December 1986. In California, New York, and Michigan, 156 observations are analyzed from January 1975 through December 1987. One of the problems in using time-series analysis is that sufficiently long baselines of data are often not available.[14] It is essential that drift, seasonality, and random variation be detected so that changes in the observations are not incorrectly attributed to the policy intervention. It is extremely difficult to model a time series with less than fifty observations prior to the intervention. The data easily conform to this criterion.

Assuming that one has a lengthy series to analyze the effects of a policy intervention, other problems remain. The most crucial one is that it usually is incorrect to analyze time-series data with ordinary least squares (OLS) regression. While

OLS regression assumes that the error term in a given equation is uncorrelated over time, time-series data frequently violate this assumption. While estimation problems usually do not occur with regard to the regression coefficients, the more serious problem is with the tests of statistical significance. Bias is likely in the standard errors of the regression coefficients because of a tendency of serial dependence (autocorrelation) in a series, which can result in the inflation of *t*-scores used to calculate significance tests. Thus with OLS, one may falsely conclude that a given policy has a significant effect.

To minimize these problems in estimating program effects, I use a regression based upon autoregressive integrated moving average (ARIMA) models.[15] The estimation procedure was generated through the ARIMA routine of the Statistical Analysis System.[16] Basically, the models consist of straight regression estimates of each policy intervention, corrected for autocorrelation in the series.[17] Estimates for each of the interventions are presented in the appendix.[18]

# 4

## *BRITISH TRAFFIC SAFETY REFORMS*

*GREAT BRITAIN* has been in the forefront of attempts to reform traffic behavior since the 1960s, when the breathalyzer was introduced. While policy developments and the passage of significant legislation moved slowly during the 1970s, the 1980s saw two significant interventions. These are the 1983 seat belt law and the December 1983 Christmas Crusade against drunk drivers.[1]

The British seat belt law, effective 31 January 1983, is important in that it preceded the passage of similar statutes in the United States. The first seat belt law in America, passed in New York, was was effective beginning 1 January 1985. Since the implementation of the New York law, a majority of states have passed legislation, and despite relatively low compliance some of the laws have had significant impacts. In contrast, in Great Britain, compliance is high and the data provide an opportunity to view the effects of a mandatory use law under ideal conditions. In addition, Britain provides an opportunity to examine the implementation of a crusade against drinking drivers.

While these interventions have been analyzed in isolation,[2] they have not before this been considered simultaneously; this chapter provides a comparison of a preventive and morally neutral intervention, the seat belt law, against a deterrence-based campaign against drinking and driving, the Christmas Crusade.

I proceed by describing the seat belt law and the Christmas Crusade, discussing previous attempts to reform traffic behavior in Commonwealth nations, and presenting the research design and methodology and the data analysis. Finally, the policy implications of the case for deterrence theory and traffic safety are explored.

## *TRAFFIC REFORM IN 1983*

### *The Seat Belt Law*

The 1983 seat belt law was added as a provision of the Road Traffic Act of 1972. It was approved by Parliament in August 1982, after some debate. As in the United States, many in Britain who opposed the law made their case on the grounds of civil liberties, but they ultimately were unsuccessful.[3] In addition to the requirement that all cars manufactured after June 1964 be equipped with seat belts or have them installed, the key provision of the law is as follows:

> Each person who drives a particular seat in any of certain motor vehicles must wear a seat belt unless he is the holder of a valid certificate signed by a registered medical practitioner to the effect that it is inadvisable on medical grounds for him to wear a seat belt or falls within certain other exceptions.[4]

The practical interpretation of the law is that wearing the seat belt is compulsory for drivers and passengers in the front seat of automobiles and light vans. In addition to persons with medical problems, those who are exempt include local delivery roundsmen and drivers who are reversing.[5] Responsibility for wearing the belt rests with individual passengers and not with the vehicle driver. In comparison to the laws passed in American states, the financial penalty is severe. The routine fine is fifty pounds, which translates into approximately seventy-five U.S. dollars. In the United States, the Department of Transportation recommends that state seat belt laws have a minimum fine of twenty-five dollars. Many states have not met this figure, and no state is near the British level of penalty unless multiple infractions occur. In Britain, as in the United States, drivers are not penalized with points on the license for failure to obey the seat belt law.[6]

Perhaps in part because of the heavy financial penalty, there was an appreciable increase in seat belt use following the enactment of the British law. Department of Transportation roadside surveys establish that the use of the device was in the range of 30 to 40 percent during the late 1970s and early 1980s. After implementation of the law, compliance has varied between 93 and 97 percent.[7] Even though initial enforcement was lax in some areas, compliance was high.[8] Accordingly, any lack of impact of the law on injury and death cannot be attributed to not wearing the belts.

## *The Christmas Crusade*

The Christmas Crusade against drinking and driving resulted in a significant decline in crash-related fatalities during December 1983. Curiously, while a reduction was experienced for all fatalities, it was not evident in the nighttime.[9] The crusade was not centrally coordinated by the British government but rather was the consequence of a number of coincidental events during or preceding December 1983. For example, throughout 1983 a number of drivers had appealed drunk-driving charges under a new evidential breath-testing procedure. On 9 December a court ruling permitted a resumption of postponed cases, and a backlog of citizens were convicted at this time.

But most important, the Department of Transportation in

December conducted its annual campaign against drinking and driving. The media helped publicize the campaign, and several local constabularies (such as in Nottinghamshire) greatly increased enforcement. Police detention for drunken drivers became more commonplace. For example, in the suburb of Grays, outside London, magistrates used a little known provision of the law that permitted them to lock up defendants in police cells for up to four days. Before this time, the jail alternative was not used for routine drinking and driving cases. While the judicial policy existed before the Christmas Crusade and continued after it, the fact that it came into focus in December 1983 greatly added to the momentum against drinking and driving.

Although increased severity of punishment was one element of the publicity campaign, the Christmas Crusade increased certainty of apprehension and punishment. Research indicates that where enforcement is increased substantially, such as by more intensive patrolling, there is some tendency for alcohol-related accidents to decline. A study of the 1975 experiment in the Midlands county of Cheshire, where the chief constable intensified breath testing for alcohol in the late night hours, reveals a decline in serious and fatal injuries. The reduction in night casualties was stronger than for those during the day. Again, the brevity of the time period of stricter enforcement resulted in a short-term effect of the law.[10]

While both of the interventions analyzed here took place in 1983, they are sufficiently separated in time that their effects on fatalities and serious accidents are independent.

## *PRIOR RESEARCH ON TRAFFIC SAFETY IN THE BRITISH COMMONWEALTH*

Much work on the effects of mandatory seat belt use have been conducted in Commonwealth nations, and most show a decline in casualties associated with the passage of legislation.

New Zealand legislated compulsory seat belt use for front seat riders on 1 January 1972. Analysis of this experience suggests that seat belt use reduced the probability of fatal injury in a given crash by about 40 percent.[11] Those who did not use the seat belt after passage of the law are in a particularly high risk group, for whom "increased belt use would result in disproportionate savings."[12]

A study of seat belt use in Victoria, Australia, documents a reduction in severe or fatal injuries after passage of the December 1970 law.[13] However, there was an increase in minor injuries, particularly to the thorax, lower torso, and neck (whiplash). The increase in minor injuries was not a result of potentially severe injuries being made less serious because of seat belt use. Rather, the minor injuries resulted from wearing the belt. This would explain the upward trend in whiplash injuries. Despite these findings, one must be cautious in concluding that there is an increase in the possibility of minor injuries following the passage of a seat belt law: the law decreases the likelihood of both fatal crashes and serious crashes. This fact makes minor injuries more likely.

A key problem in the Commonwealth with the implementation of seat belt laws is compliance. For example, compliance with seat belt laws in the Canadian provinces increased from 20 to 70 percent immediately after the passage of the law but then dropped to about 50 percent during the next few years.[14] It is perhaps because of declining compliance that no consistent reduction in fatalities and injuries across provinces was demonstrated. Seat belt legislation may fall short of expectations because primarily drivers who already drive safely comply with these laws. Recently, compliance in Canada has improved greatly because of increased publicity and enforcement, but the literature also demonstrates the difficulty of changing the habits of Canadians.[15]

While compliance with the British law was high, a panel survey demonstrates that before the effective date of the legislation those who wore the seat belt were separated from non-users by socioeconomic status, gender, and general healthful behavior.[16] Females and citizens with good health habits and higher socioeconomic status were more inclined to use the seat belt. After legislation was passed, the difference disappeared for all but the socioeconomic groups. However, all groups increased seat belt use after the law. In short, as intended, the legislation itself seemed to increase use across the population.

Most attempts at reforming drinking and driving are based on the traditional concept of criminal deterrence, which

> proposes that the efficacy of a legal threat is a function of the perceived certainty, severity, and swiftness or celerity of punishment in the event of a violation of the law. The greater the perceived likelihood of apprehension, conviction, and punishment, the more severe the perceived eventual penalty, and the more swiftly it is perceived to be administered, the greater will be the deterrent effect of the threat.[17]

Studies of the attempts to introduce breath testing systematically in Canada, Australia, and New Zealand conclude that the new laws had, at best, a temporary effect on traffic casualties.[18] As in Britain, the reason for the weak effects of the legislation is that, initially, citizens overestimate the probability of apprehension and temporarily change their behavior. Once they realize that chances for arrest are much lower than they had thought, drivers return to their normal patterns.

The effects of drinking and driving reforms in the Commonwealth nations are weak partly because apprehension is not certain and punishment is not swift. The Christmas Crusade in Britain allows us to view not only more severe and swifter punishment but also increased certainty of apprehension. Although increased police patrol (or blitzes) did not occur in every section of England and Wales, Department of

Transportation publicity about them went out to the entire nation. Similarly, while immediate lockup was the exception rather than the rule, the jailings in Grays received widespread attention. Such publicity could have deterred British drivers during this period.

## *DATA AND METHODOLOGY*

Data were collected by the Department of Transportation from January 1977 through December 1986. For all variables, 120 observations were examined. February 1983 was the first postintervention month for the seat belt; thus, 47 postintervention and 73 preintervention observations were used. December 1983 was the primary month of the Christmas Crusade; data are available only for England and Wales.

The primary dependent variable of interest is the number of fatalities and serious car casualties. For the U.S. states discussed in this book, only fatalities are used. Reported injuries in the U.S. Fatal Accident Reporting System are those that occur in conjunction with a fatal accident; injury data bases gathered separately by the states often are not comparable. In contrast, data are available in England and Wales that include injuries regardless of whether or not a fatality occurred. Since the primary interest in this chapter is the effectiveness of seat belt legislation, the examination of injuries enriches the data base and allows for systematic control comparisons. The difference between serious and nonserious casualties is a bit arbitrary; the Department of Transportation defines serious casualties as those that involve either hospitalization or fracture, internal injury, concussion, crushing, or severe general shock. To be counted as a fatal accident, the death must occur within thirty days of the crash.[19]

Since the literature demonstrates that there usually is a reduction in fatal and serious casualties following the passage of seat belt legislation, I hypothesize that there should be a statistically significant decline in the series after January 1983. In accordance with the hypothesis developed in chapter 2, the high compliance evident in Britain suggests that the law should be effective throughout the postintervention period.

I also expect a significant decline in the second dependent variable—nonserious car casualties—following the intervention, although the effect of the law may not be as strong as in the case of the fatal and serious casualties. The reason is this: while a seat belt can reduce serious injury and death, it cannot prevent the accidents themselves or the many minor injuries that result from them. It is my guess that there is considerable potential for an accident to change from fatal or serious categories to the nonserious category, for the seat belt can prevent only casualties, not accidents. This could cause the number of nonserious casualties to increase after the intervention.

Although the interrupted time series is a powerful research design, provided one can rule out alternative explanations, much of the literature recommends a control series where possible.[20] For the exploration of the British experience, I chose two nonequivalent control series. The first consists of fatal and serious casualties from highway accidents involving buses, trucks, two-wheeled motor vehicles, pedestrians, and bicycles. The second control consists of nonserious casualties involving the same transportation modes. Both controls are compared to the two treatment series. As seat belt legislation applies only to automobile drivers and passengers in the front seat, one would not expect a similar reduction in casualties in accidents involving other motor vehicles or pedestrians. More likely, noncar accidents will follow their pattern of gradual decline, which they have demonstrated since the early 1960s.

In contrast to the hypothesized effect of the seat belt, one would not expect the impact of the Christmas Crusade to last. Accordingly, I tested for a temporary decline in casualties for this intervention. The reason for expecting the temporary change was because of the crusade's brevity and the unique chain of events surrounding it. In addition, one might not expect the crusade to have a strong impact on automobiles, because if the seat belt law is especially powerful, it may overwhelm the other intervention. On the other hand, since vehicles in the control series are not covered by the seat belt law, one may expect the crusade to have an impact on these groups.

## *ANALYSIS OF THE REFORMS*

The trend of serious and fatal traffic casualties is displayed in figure 1. To minimize seasonal variation, the data are presented as a twelve-month moving average. It is apparent that there is a striking drop in the series in February 1983, following the implementation of the seat belt law. If one compares the trend line after the intervention to the preintervention trend line, the fatalities decline by 18.1 percent, an average of 453.51 fatal and serious casualties per month. (The estimates of the interventions are presented in the appendix).[21] The series does tend to rise slightly beginning in early 1984. Since compliance has been constant in England and Wales, perhaps the rise is due to increased travel. Still, through 1986 the overall level of the series continues to be lower than in previous years.

As expected, the impact of the Christmas Crusade was not as lasting as that of the seat belt, although the drop in December 1983 is statistically significant. While I was unable to find a permanent effect of the crusade beyond December, that month experienced a 17.9 percent decline in serious and fatal casualties over and above the effects produced by the seat belt law.

I did not expect a similar reduction in death and injury for the control series—fatal and serious noncar highway casual-

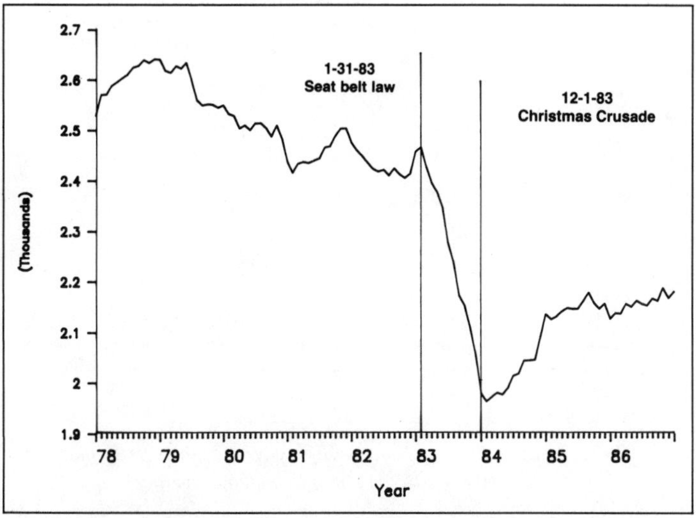


FIGURE 1. *Fatal or Serious Car Casualties in England and Wales, 1977–1986 (12-month moving average)*

ties. Figure 2 shows a much more gradual decline in the trend line over the entire period. The break in the series immediately after the intervention is much less sharp and distinct than in figure 1. Still, reduction appears in the long term. The law's introduction may have made all drivers more cautious and the intervention may have had some temporary spillover effect to drivers of trucks and buses. The law may also have made all drivers more conscious of police presence.[22] In any event, the pattern for car fatalities and serious injuries indicates a much stronger reduction.

The effect of the seat belt law also is doubtful on nonserious car casualties (figure 3). Only a very slight change is apparent after the first few months of the intervention, followed by a sharper downward shift later in 1983. Comparison of the preintervention and postintervention trend lines reveals that

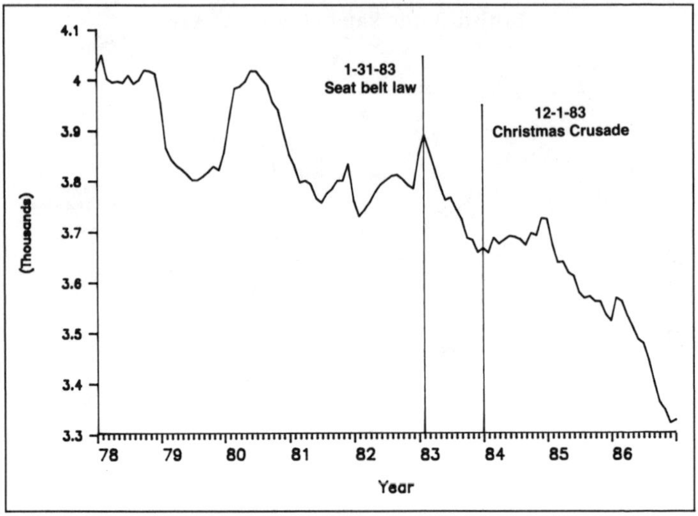


FIGURE 2. *Fatal or Serious Noncar Highway Casualties in England and Wales, 1977–1986 (12-month moving average)*

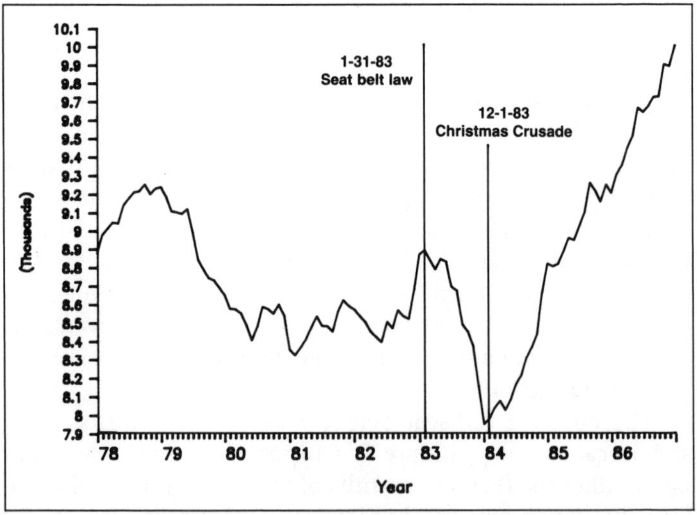


FIGURE 3. *Nonserious Car Casualties in England and Wales, 1977–1986 (12-month moving average)*

the change is not significant over the long term. The increase in the series beginning in 1984 is possibly the consequence of potential serious and fatal casualties becoming nonserious after the introduction of the seat belt legislation. The effect of the Christmas Crusade on automobile occupants was a casualty reduction of 13.8 percent for December 1983. Again, in reducing nonserious casualties temporarily, the crackdown appears to have benefited car drivers, the most likely social drinkers.

Finally, I examined nonserious, noncar highway casualties. Although there is a higher number of casualties overall, figure 4 is a mirror of figure 2. The trend line declines following the intervention but the overall reduction is not as marked visually as figure 3. The reduction beginning in February 1983 again may indicate that all drivers became more cautious of

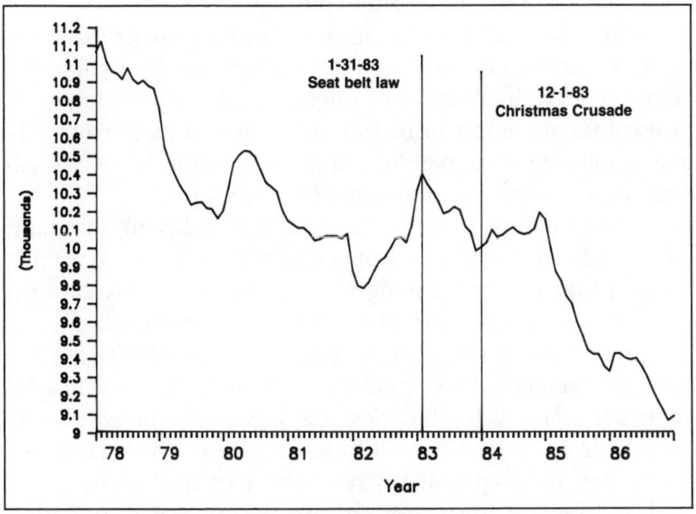


FIGURE 4. *Nonserious Noncar Highway Casualties in England and Wales, 1977–1986 (12-month moving average)*

police vigilance or drove more safely because of publicity surrounding the seat belt legislation. On average, there was a greater reduction in the nonserious, noncar highway casualties than in casualties involving automobiles, but the shift seems due more to a declining trend than to the seat belt law itself.

## *ALTERNATIVE EXPLANATIONS*

The 1983 seat belt law and the Christmas Crusade had the greatest impact on serious and fatal traffic casualties. But as the literature on drinking and driving indicates, there frequently are a number of alternative explanations to automobile safety interventions, which must be considered to insure it is the policy itself and not outside factors that have the primary effect on the dependent variable.[23] Thus, a few rival explanations are worth exploring.

A first alternative explanation is the changing British economy, which experienced high unemployment throughout this time. I added the number of unemployed to the equations to control for the effect of recession and found its impact to be negligible (see the appendix). Moreover, results were virtually unchanged when unemployment was removed.

A second explanation is the amount of driving that takes place. If driving suddenly dropped beginning in 1983, we may suspect that reduced driving is an alternative explanation of the lower number of casualties. But data from the Department of Transportation reveal that for cars, taxis and light vans, the total kilometers driven actually increased annually from 1982 to 1986; motorcycles, bicycles, and buses also increased kilometers driven but at a slightly lesser rate.[24] So it seems unlikely that reduced traffic played any part in the lower fatal and serious car casualties in the postintervention period. Moreover, the case for the effectiveness of the seat belt law is greatly strengthened by the fact that kilometers of travel for cars and taxis rose from 208.77 billion in 1982 to 297.65 billion in 1986.[25] This trend helps to account for the slight increase in slope for fatal and serious car casualties observed through 1986. So despite a much higher volume of travel two and three years after the intervention, fatalities and serious injuries still stayed below the preintervention series. Thus, the rate of death and serious injury was reduced considerably.[26]

A third factor is liquor consumption and, more important, decrease in the number of persons drinking and driving. Consumption data for Great Britain as a whole reveal that production of spirits from 1982 through 1984 dropped; however, the amount released for home consumption rose, as did the amount of spirits imported from elsewhere. In addition, beer and wine drinking increased.[27] On the more important question of drinking while driving, evidence suggests that, after an initial drop following the introduction of the breathalyzer in 1967, the percentage of drivers killed in road accidents with blood alcohol above the prescribed limit (80 milligrams of alcohol per 100 milliliters of blood) rose steadily throughout the 1970s. There was some reduction in this figure from 1982 to 1983; however, the fall in the data appears occasioned more from a steep rise during 1982 than a declining trend over the years. While some of the reduction in serious casualties and fatalities in 1983 could have been due to less drinking and driving, the percentage of drivers killed with high blood alcohol levels was roughly the same in 1983 as at the beginning of the series in 1977.[28] Moreover, use of the breathalyzer was relatively constant over the years, with the number of persons involved in accidents who failed the test ranging from roughly 9,500 to 12,000, with slight reductions from 1982 to 1984.[29]

But it also is possible that the seat belt law reduced the casualties in the accidents caused by drinking drivers. Many people killed in alcohol-related accidents are themselves drunk drivers, and reform measures like the seat belt "must necessarily save drunks, and evenhanded victim-assistance programs will have as principal beneficiaries the same law-violators whose anti-social behavior is otherwise blasted and condemned."[30] In order to explore the possibility that the seat belt law saved drunken drivers from injury and death, I examined the number of fatal and serious accidents on Friday and Saturday nights from 9 P.M. until 6 A.M. Although this indicator does not directly measure the consequences of alcohol-impaired driving, it has been used as a surrogate variable in studies that examine the effects of drunk-driving laws.[31] Also, it provides an opportunity to test for the effects of the Christmas Crusade with more sensitive data.[32]

I found good support for the seat belt hypothesis. Figure 5

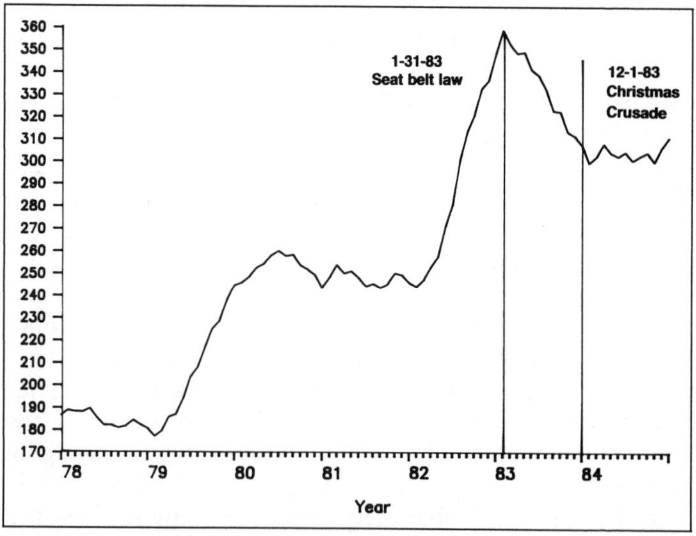


FIGURE 5. *Fatal or Serious Single-Vehicle Car Accidents in England and Wales, Weekend Nights, 1977–1984 (12-month moving average)*

indicates a permanent drop in the first postintervention month, a drop that was maintained throughout the entire postintervention series. The figure suggests that, rather than a lower drunken-driving rate reducing accidents, the seat belt law reduced fatal and serious single-vehicle accidents in the late night weekend hours—a time when alcohol-related crashes are most likely to occur. Overall, a statistically significant 41.4 percent reduction was observed in the postintervention series.

So in addition to affecting all drivers favorably, the seat belt law appears to reduce the probability of injury or death from drinking drivers, a particularly high-risk group for accidents. In addition, aggregate data for Great Britain point to the efficacy of the new legislation. Of those slightly injured in car accidents during 1983, 93 percent wore the seat belt. This percentage was 89 and 79 percent for those seriously injured and killed, respectively. The corresponding figures for 1984 are 97, 94 and 85 percent, respectively.[33]

In contrast to expectation, the effect of the Christmas Crusade on these drivers was insignificant. The finding was a strong and temporary reduction for all fatalities but not for the night hours.[34] Thus the data indicate that the seat belt may have more lasting value in saving lives than a temporary crackdown on drinking and driving.

## *DISCUSSION*

If we return to the theoretical framework presented in chapter 2, the traditional deterrence model of drinking and driving fits the British data well. The Christmas Crusade reduced total fatalities and serious casualties only temporarily. It is difficult to change British behavior over the long term because the custom of drinking and driving has considerable popular support.

To determine whether the effects of the seat belt law are

permanent, data must be evaluated continually in future years. While the postintervention series is lower than previously, some deterioration in impact is evident visually through 1986. One possibility, which with increases in kilometers driven may help explain the upward rise in fatal and serious casualties, is the fact that the law applies only to those riding in the front seat; casualties have not declined for back seat passengers.[35] Consequently, an obvious strategy to improve the effectiveness of the law is to make the belts mandatory for all passengers.

The experience of seat belt legislation in England and Wales has important implications for the United States and other Western nations where the primary emphasis until recently for saving lives on the highways has been curbing drunken driving.[36] Among the possible reasons why the seat belt law in Britain seems to effect a more striking change than the Christmas Crusade is that the law takes a broader and more even-handed approach to traffic safety.[37] With the seat belt, traffic safety is not viewed as a problem for the few who violate the law. Rather, safety is seen as a general problem, with important benefits to all if addressed successfully. Drinking and driving experiments seem to fail when there is limited recognition of the pervasiveness of the traffic safety problem. Options other than individual deterrence are seldom pursued. These other options include limiting alcohol availability, raising alcohol prices and taxes, executing alcohol-related transportation policies, and limiting alcohol advertising.[38] In fact, government can at times actually encourage drinking and driving by permitting the location of bars, nightclubs, and state liquor stores on interstate highways.[39]

Among the important factors in changing a custom is the utilitarian and moral significance of the custom to its adher ents.[40] In combating drinking and driving, the utilitarian aspects of the event seem to outweigh the negative moral connotations, at least in England and Wales. One of the advantages of seat belt legislation is that, compared to drinking and driving legislation, it is morally neutral. Punishment and criminality are minimized, and the desirability of safety for the entire society is emphasized. It is not surprising, therefore, that the evidence suggests that seat belt legislation has an effect on late night and weekend casualties. Accidents during these periods are the ones most likely to involve alcohol. The solution to the drinking and driving problem ultimately must be approached from interventions other than the seat belt. However, the device appears to have some potential to reduce injury and death that drunk drivers inflict upon themselves and others.

# 5

## *HIGHWAY SAFETY IN NEW YORK STATE*

*

NEW YORK is one of the most innovative states in traffic safety reform. While the British case involves only two policy interventions, New York is more complex. By raising the minimum legal drinking age, passing stricter laws to deal with drinking drivers and having the first mandatory seat belt use law in the United States, New York set examples that other states adopted rapidly. As with other states, while a number of studies have evaluated some of these reforms in isolation, almost no work has analyzed the combined effects of these interventions.

The purpose of this chapter is to examine the effects of four traffic safety reforms in New York State: the 28 November 1981 law that standardized and increased penalties for drinking and driving; the legislation that went into effect on 1 December 1982, raising the legal drinking age from eighteen to nineteen; the mandatory seat belt use law, effective 1 January 1985; and the legislation raising the drinking age from nineteen to twenty-one, effective 1 December 1985. I will proceed by reviewing these traffic safety reforms; presenting the research design, methodology, and data analysis; and discussing the theoretical relevance and policy implications of these efforts.

## TRAFFIC SAFETY REFORM

Concern in New York State over the physical and emotional trauma caused by drinking drivers gained impetus in the late 1970s. In December 1979, Governor Hugh Carey appointed a task force on drunken drinking, headed by Dr. Shelia E. Blume, director of the New York State Division of Drug Abuse and James P. Melton, Commissioner of Motor Vehicles.[1] Largely because of the task force's recommendations, legislative action began in the early 1980s. In July 1980 Governor Carey signed three bills increasing penalties for driving while impaired by alcohol or drugs, but those measures, effective in September of that year, were relatively mild.[2] For example, first offenders driver's licenses were suspended for 90 instead of the 60 days. For a second conviction, they were suspended for 180 days instead of 120. While plea bargaining was made more limited, judges retained considerable discretion.

In 1982 legislation was passed allowing police to arrest drinking drivers who violated the law on private property or on access roads.[3] As in many states, a loophole existed for violations on private property prior to the law. At the same time, Carey signed a bill providing for mandatory license revocation for a second impaired-driving offense.[4] (Impaired driving is driving with a blood-alcohol concentration between 0.05 and 0.099, while driving while intoxicated [DWI] is driving with a concentration of 0.10 or greater.) In 1983, Governor Cuomo signed legislation creating two new categories of crime—vehicular manslaughter and vehicular assault—which consist of causing death or serious injury when driving a vehicle while legally intoxicated.[5]

### The 1981 DWI Reform

While all of these laws may have had some effect on casualties, they received little publicity and public awareness seemed low. The most significant legislation is the package passed by the State Assembly and signed by Governor Carey in August 1981. The law took effect on 28 November of the same year. The governor declared, "The right to drive a motor vehicle is not absolute. The bills which I am approving today establish a comprehensive program to remove incapacitated drivers from the highways of our state."[6] The law has the following key provisions.

1. The driver's license is suspended immediately and automatically if there are two alcohol-related driving offenses within three years.
2. For first offenders, a $250 fine is mandated if the driver is impaired and $350 if the driver's blood-alcohol concentration is over the 0.10 limit. In addition, judges have the power to imprison first offenders, although the prison option is not often used for this group.
3. Fines and sentences become progressively more severe as violations increase. For those who commit three alcohol violations within a ten year period, imprisonment can last up to six months and fines can be as high as $1,500. In addition, for a second offense with a blood-alcohol concentration greater than 0.10, a felony conviction is possible.
4. Finally, those convicted of driving with a revoked or suspended license are subject to a mandatory jail sentence between 7 and 180 days as well as a fine between $200 and $500.

Judges are prohibited from discharging cases without imposing at least the minimum fines for any of the above violations. Since the passage of the law, even a first offense is not routinely plea bargained if the accused has a blood alcohol level of 0.15 or above.[7] In addition, the plea bargain is more difficult if an accident is involved. The stricter penalties have, however, given rise to a problem—the number of trials for alcohol-related traffic offenses has risen drastically.[8]

In short, the New York State law both standardizes the

penalties for drinking and driving and accentuates the possibility of imprisonment. The new laws are known collectively as Special Traffic Options Programs Against Driving While Intoxicated (STOP-DWI). Spurred by the publicity efforts of such groups as Mothers Against Drunk Driving (MADD) and by public opinion in favor of cracking down on drinking drivers, police enforcement was vigorous. Local governments are permitted to keep a substantial portion of the fines, a fact that has gained support for both the reform and its enforcement. In 1980, the number of persons arrested for DWI stood at slightly more than 50,000. For the years 1982 through 1984, the average was close to 70,000.[9] The number of drivers sentenced to probation, which requires participation in an alcohol treatment program, doubled—from 3,598 in 1981 to 7,392 in 1985.[10]

An impact evaluation of STOP-DWI indicates an increased awareness by the public and approval of the new laws.[11] The study also demonstrates gains in apprehensions and convictions for DWI, further documenting the increase in certainty of both apprehension and punishment. The evaluation reports strong safety benefits of the law, confirming the initial optimistic assessments of public officials. Citing police reports, state officials note that alcohol-related traffic fatalities declined 32 percent from 1981 through 1984, with national figures showing only a 24 percent decline.[12]

### *The 1982 and 1985 Drinking-Age Reforms*

The second component in the strategy to reduce highway deaths is raising the drinking age. Largely because of a concern with the impact that alcohol was having on young drivers, the minimum legal drinking age was raised from eighteen to nineteen years, effective 1 December 1982. However, throughout the 1980s, both the governor's office and

Washington pressed for a higher legal age. For example, states not meeting a 1 October 1986 deadline to raise the drinking age to twenty-one faced losing 5 percent of federal highway funds during the first year and 10 percent each additional year. New York State stood to lose approximately $30 million the first year. A law mandating a minimum drinking age of twenty-one was passed by the State Legislature and signed by Governor Cuomo. It became effective on 1 December 1985.[13]

To aid compliance, colleges throughout the state limited functions and facilities for alcohol consumption. However, other factors worked against compliance. For instance, border communities had a much lower legal drinking age. Although Vermont eventually raised the legal age to twenty-one, when the New York State law was passed, its drinking age was eighteen. In Quebec and Ontario, the drinking age remains at nineteen, even though they have tougher laws against driving under the influence of alcohol. Many people, especially those affiliated with the restaurant and tavern industries, suggested that the new drinking age could cause more problems than it solved, because young people would drive further to obtain alcohol legally.[14]

Public officials maintained, however, that raising the drinking age reduces alcohol-related accidents among young drivers. In a speech before the American Automobile Association on 24 April 1986, Governor Cuomo stated, "Last December when the age at which people could drink legally was raised to 21 years, six people were killed in accidents caused by drunken drivers under 21, 10 less than in December 1984."[15] One must be cautious about accepting such figures because of the unreliability of police reports and the one point in time used; however, evidence does indicates that alcohol consumption was reduced, at least among those eighteen years of age and under, after the drinking age was changed to nineteen.[16] Accordingly, we might expect a decline in casualties.

## *The Mandatory Seat Belt Use Law*

New York's seat belt legislation took effect between the implementation of the two changes in drinking age and is separated enough in time so we may evaluate its independent effects. While the legislation became official on 1 December 1984, only warning tickets were issued during the first month. Accordingly, 1 January 1985 is used as the onset month of intervention. According to data supplied by the state to the University of North Carolina Highway Safety Research Center, seat belt use was approximately 16 percent prior to the passage of the law, rose to a high of 57 percent shortly after onset, and declined to approximately 48 percent by 1987.[17] Evidence also indicates that compliance is lowest during the night hours, a period of high accident risk.[18]

Enforcement does not seem particularly strong, judging from the data gathered by the Highway Safety Research Center. New York State has primary enforcement, meaning that a citation may be issued for simply not buckling the belt. In secondary enforcement states, another violation (such as speeding, running a red light, and so forth) must have happened before a citation can be issued. In spite of this fact, New York State does not rank high in seat belt citations per 100,000 population. During 1985–1986, the state police issued only 79 tickets per 100,000, while local police gave 314 citations per the same metric. In Ohio, a secondary enforcement state, 846 tickets were given per 100,000 citizens.

Even though enforcement and compliance are weak compared with Great Britain, a number of evaluations demonstrate considerable reductions in fatalities and other casualties following the implementation of the law for groups covered by the legislation (front seat occupants). For example, one analysis by the National Highway Traffic Safety Administration estimates that 220 fewer persons avoided death on the highway under what was forecast had there been no mandatory restraint law.[19]

By 1986, many citizens in New York State were convinced of the impact of one or more intervention. In 1985 death and serious injury to drivers was the lowest since 1949, despite increased traffic on the highways. Governor Cuomo attributed the decline to all four interventions considered in this study. "Hundreds of New Yorkers are alive today as a result of our many innovative highway safety programs. . . . I am proud that our state continues to be a national leader in the field."[20] Still unanswered is the comparative effectiveness of each intervention in improving the safety record.

## *RESEARCH DESIGN AND METHODOLOGY*

In general, I follow procedures outlined in chapter 3. To analyze the effect of the DWI reform, I compared single-vehicle nighttime male driver fatalities to all single-vehicle fatalities that occurred during the day. Also, I examined all daytime fatalities and compared them to the treatment series. For the legal drinking age, I examine the effects of the laws on the age groups for which they are intended. The effects should be stronger on these groups than on the entire population of fatalities. In examining the seat belt law, I compare those drivers covered by the law (drivers and front seat passengers) with those not covered (back seat passengers). I excluded children less than ten years old, who are covered by the New York law in the back seat.

In attempting to devise an impact model for each series, I tested for both temporary and permanent change following the interventions. This is because the literature on traffic safety suggests that laws to deter drinking drivers usually have a short-term effect, if any at all. In contrast, more abrupt and permanent changes have been documented for both drinking-age and seat belt interventions, and I developed the models accordingly.[21]

## ANALYSIS OF THE REFORMS

The first task of the data analysis is to determine any change in the trend of total fatalities due to any of the interventions. Monthly fatalities from 1975 through 1987 are presented in figure 6 in the form of a twelve-month moving average. (Estimates of the interventions are presented in the appendix.)

While the recession and a corresponding lowering of miles driven help account for a decline in the series immediately prior

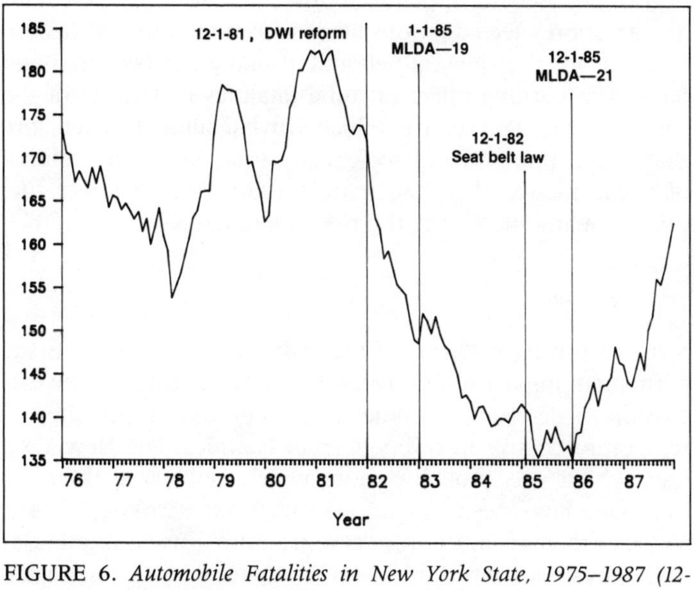


FIGURE 6. *Automobile Fatalities in New York State, 1975–1987 (12-month moving average)*

to the intervention, figure 6 demonstrates that a sharp and permanent reduction in the trend line was maintained through 1986.[22] This is against the expectation, in that traffic safety literature indicates that most similar reforms produce only a short-term drop in fatalities. The shift in the data coincides with the stricter law governing driving while intoxicated that took effect on 28 November. If one compares the trend line after the intervention to the preintervention series, total fatalities decline by 16.58 percent (an average of approximately twenty-eight fatalities per month). The impact of the two drinking-age interventions (1 December 1982 and 1 December 1985) is not apparent in the visual examination of the data (the series actually rises after December 1985), and the effect of the mandatory seat belt use law (1 January 1985) is, at best, temporary.

The ineffectiveness of these laws is confirmed through statistical tests (see the appendix); however, one must view their impact upon affected groups before accepting this conclusion. One reason why the seat belt and drinking-age laws may not have had a strong effect on total fatalities is because of the success of the DWI reform, which drove fatalities down before these other interventions took place. In addition, the volume of traffic increased in the middle 1980s due to lower fuel prices, greatly increasing the risk of accident.[23]

## *DWI Reform*

Most surprising in terms of the traffic safety literature is the permanent impact of the DWI reform. As indicated in the discussion of deterrence, studies in Britain and France show a temporary change in the pattern of fatalities. The New York law, which was probably more widely publicized than the European laws, seems to have a much more striking impact. In order to confirm the results more fully, I use a number of nonequivalent control groups to compare with the aggregate fatalities. The literature demonstrates that accidents involving alcohol are more likely to occur at night and to involve a single vehicle with a male driver. This series was contrasted with single-vehicle fatalities for both males and females during the day and with all daytime fatalities. It was reasoned that since daytime accidents are less likely to involve alcohol, the effects of the 1981 DWI reform may be weaker during this period. Data presented in figures 7–9 confirm this hypothesis.

Overall, there is a significant and permanent reduction for single-vehicle fatalities for males during the nighttime hours following the DWI intervention. Moreover, the effect of the law at night is stronger than when all automobile fatalities are considered. An average of 8.58 lives are saved per month, a 27.4 percent decrease under the preintervention series. The seat

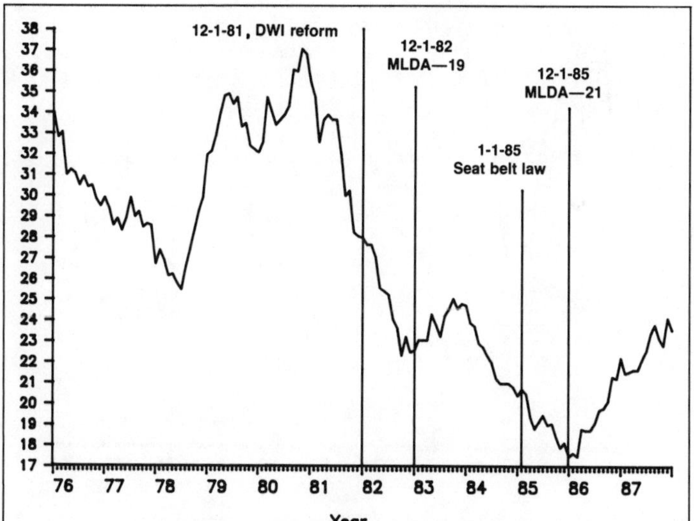


FIGURE 7. *Single-Vehicle Fatalities in New York State, Male Drivers, Nighttime, 1975–1987 (12-month moving average)*

belt intervention is also effective when nighttime fatalities involving single vehicles and male drivers are examined. The decrease for the postintervention series is 12.2 percent. This finding conflicts with some empirical literature that suggests that seat belt use in New York State tends to be lower at night than in the day.[24] The greater likelihood of fatalities and serious accidents occurring during the period might help account for the greater effectiveness of the seat belt. For example, the previous chapter demonstrates that the seat belt reduces serious and fatal injuries more than minor injuries.

One-car daytime fatalities (figure 8) and all daytime fatal accidents (figure 9) do not respond as strongly to the DWI

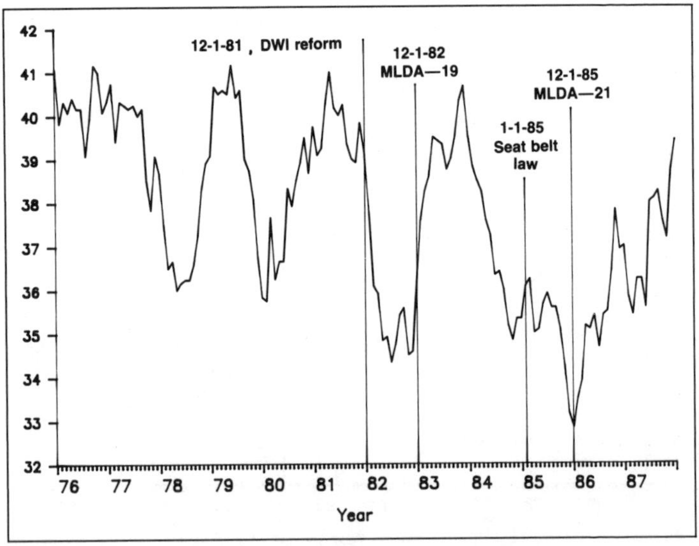


FIGURE 8. *Single-Vehicle Fatalities in New York State, All Drivers, Daytime, Weekdays, 1975–1987 (12-month moving average)*

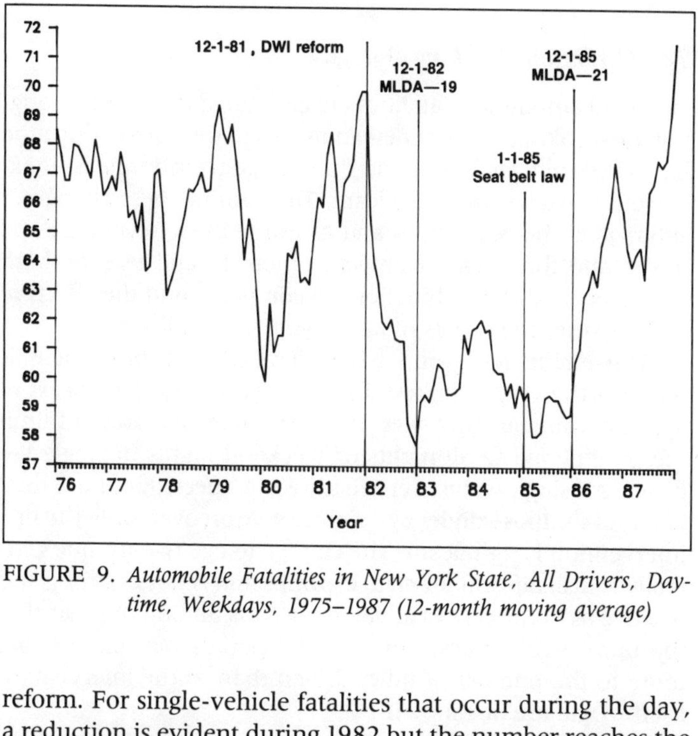


FIGURE 9. *Automobile Fatalities in New York State, All Drivers, Daytime, Weekdays, 1975–1987 (12-month moving average)*

reform. For single-vehicle fatalities that occur during the day, a reduction is evident during 1982 but the number reaches the level of the preintervention series during 1983. Clearly, the law's effect is less permanent than for similar fatalities at night with a male driver. A more striking reduction is evident for all daytime fatalities, but the decline under the preintervention series is 16.3 percent, still well below the 27 percent drop at night for fatalities in accidents involving single vehicles and male drivers. The continued (if weaker) impact of the DWI reform during the day is probably due to the strength and publicity of the law. Also, while most drinking and driving occurs at night, probably a considerable amount happens during the day. These fatalities also may have been affected by the law.

### *The Minimum Drinking-Age Law*

When all automobile fatalities are examined (figure 6), changing the drinking age to nineteen moves in the correct direction but is insignificant, while the shift to age twenty-one is unexpectedly positive and significant. To examine these changes, I subdivided the population and examine those seventeen and under and those aged eighteen, nineteen, and twenty, both separately and in combination. In comparison to the effects of DWI reform, the effects of age changes are still weak.

The major age group where a positive improvement is found is the very youngest drivers—those seventeen years of age and younger. However, the law is effective only if I limit the time period to all nights or weekend nights in single vehicles. All single-vehicle crashes are not affected, nor are total fatalities for those under age eighteen. Moreover, only the first intervention is significant. The change to age twenty-one generally is insignificant for all age groups and is not as strong and positive as in the case of all fatalities. This finding suggests that the number of fatalities in the total population may be due more to the number of miles driven than to the intervention itself. (Data are not shown.)

It is difficult to make a case for the minimum drinking age, because the change to age nineteen occurred only a year after a more powerful DWI intervention in New York. The 1981 DWI reform was passed not only to punish drunk drivers but also to reduce fatalities among young drivers, who are especially prone to alcohol-related traffic accidents. By the time the drinking age rose to age twenty-one (December 1985), New York State already had experienced seat belts, DWI reform, and a change in the drinking age to nineteen. Given the power of the DWI law and the seat belt reform, it may have been difficult to reduce fatalities much further by 1986.

Another reason for the comparatively low impact of the drinking-age laws is the unique licensing situation for young drivers in New York State. For drivers under age eighteen, driving during the night hours is not permitted unless the youth successfully completes a high school driver education course. In New York City and its suburb of Nassau County, no licenses are issued to drivers under eighteen unless a driver education course is passed; in such a case, full driving privileges are granted at age seventeen. Such restriction can delay a decision to seek a license, causing fatalities to stay low.[25]

Further, New York has a curfew and New York students are aware of the curfew laws (more than students in Louisiana, another curfew state).[26] Night crashes are fewer in New York than in Louisiana as a result of these laws.[27]

As a final step, I test the hypothesis that those recently attaining majority age are affected adversely by the drinking-age laws and find no evidence of such impact. (Data are not shown.)

### *The Seat Belt Law*

I refine the analysis of seat belt legislation by comparing occupants covered by the law (those in the front seat) to passengers not covered. I divide the population accordingly and estimate seat belt effects, expecting that the law will have its greatest impact on those riding in the front seat. The analysis demonstrates an average savings of 7.30 lives per month in the front seat, a figure equivalent to a 7.8 percent reduction under the preintervention level. In contrast, the change for passengers in the back seat is not statistically significant. This finding confirms the beneficial effect of mandatory seat belt use in that it reduces fatalities primarily among those most affected by the reform.

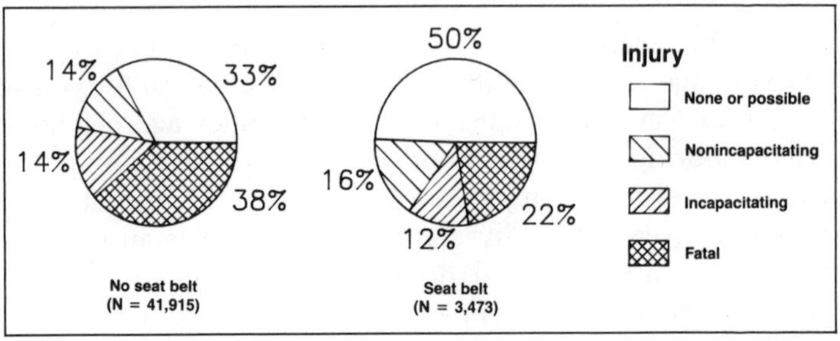


FIGURE 10. *Severity of Injuries With and Without Seat Belts, New York State, Front Seat Occupants Age Five Years or Older Involved in Fatal Accidents, 1985–1986*

Finally, I examine the general efficacy of the seat belt by dividing fatalities and injuries in fatal accidents into those wearing and those not wearing a seat belt. Data on these groups are presented in figure 10. Children four years of age and under are excluded because they are covered by a child restraint law. The finding is that those not wearing seat belts have a much greater chance of death; those wearing seat belts are much more likely to escape injury completely. The differences in injuries are slight, but with such a large population, they are statistically significant and favor those wearing seat belts.

## *DISCUSSION*

Figures 6–9 indicate a rise in fatalities beginning in 1986 and a more striking increase in 1987. A number of explanations have been advanced for the upward trend, including an increase in miles driven, a decrease in seat belt use, difficulty in getting "problem" drinkers off the road, and violation of the maintained fifty-five-mile-per-hour speed limit.[28]

Despite recent trends, a number of important conclusions emerge from the New York experience, some of which challenge the propositions about deterrence presented in chapter 2. Most significantly, and in contrast to the experience in England and Wales, the December 1981 DWI reform demonstrates that the effects of a strong law against drinking and driving combined with consistent police enforcement and support from the judiciary and local governments are not necessarily short-term. The reduction in fatalities is not due to decreased driving; in fact, the number of miles driven increased throughout this period.

Also, it seems unlikely that fatality reductions are due to a sudden decrease in the consumption of alcohol. For example, during the period surrounding the debate over drinking and driving in New York State, annual beer consumption per capita steadily increased, from 21.9 gallons in 1979 to 22.7 in 1982.[29] While the consumption of spirits declined during this period, it is probably not the cause of the drop in fatalities. A decline in liquor drinking began early in the 1970s and during much of this time fatalities increased or stayed constant.

More problematic is attributing the results exclusively to the law itself and not to the publicity surrounding its passage. But the drop in fatalities is so abrupt following December 1981 that it seems unlikely that prelaw publicity contributed to the drop. In addition, public outcry over drinking and driving and more supportive public attitudes help maintain the gains achieved by the law.

Still, preventive interventions, such as mandatory seat belt use and the changes in the drinking age, also improve road safety. While the DWI reform is the key factor in lowering fatalities, seat belt and drinking-age laws help to keep them low. Although fewer persons in New York State than in England and Wales accept the seat belt as a beneficial device, the New York case illustrates that, in addition to responding to deterrence, some citizens can become convinced of the benefits of government interventions.

The specific findings with regard to the New York seat belt law are similar to the results in England and Wales, although they are less striking. For states yet to consider passage of a mandatory use law, the analysis indicates that such legislation may reduce fatalities. The full potential of the seat belt to save lives has yet to be realized in the United States because many citizens fail to follow the law. Two approaches may be useful, one the carrot and the other the stick. Using a softer approach, government should educate the public about the benefits of seat belts. This has been attempted in many states, but a substantial proportion of citizens do not or will not hear the message. Survey research shows that lower-income, less educated people are least likely to wear the seat belt, and these possibly are the citizens most at risk.[30] In New York State, lower compliance is found among teenagers.[31] Perhaps education and information need to be targeted upon those groups.

As for the harsher approach, states currently considering a seat belt law should opt for primary enforcement. The effects of increased fines are debatable and may be a hardship on lower-income citizens, but police are badly handicapped in enforcement of the seat belt law if they can issue citations only in the case of another violation or an accident. Indeed, research in California and Michigan (secondary enforcement states) described in subsequent chapters shows much weaker results of their seat belt laws. Another alternative is to penalize drivers with points on the license if they or fellow passengers do not buckle the belt. Finally, basic research must be undertaken to determine why compliance is so poor in the United States and Canada compared to Great Britain and other European nations where nearly all citizens obey the seat belt law.[32]

The most disappointing results are with regard to the drinking-age reforms, even though a significant change is found for the very youngest male drivers in some circumstances. A number of factors may be at work. For one, the number of fatalities is so small in these age ranges that it is difficult to determine the law's precise impact. No doubt, the curfew and license restrictions help keep these figures low. Second, it is possible that the 1981 DWI reform so drastically lowered fatalities among the youngest age groups that, by the time the drinking-age changes were implemented in 1982 and 1985 (after the seat belt law), the opportunity for the statistics to improve was limited. A final note is that New York State took a gradual approach in implementing drinking-age changes, in contrast to Michigan, which abruptly increased the drinking age from eighteen to twenty-one in 1978, with highly favorable results.[33] It appears that, in accordance with federal policy, the legal drinking age is likely to remain at age twenty-one for some time; but to ascertain the effectiveness of policy shifts, a sharp rather than a gradual change may be the preferred approach.

In sum, government efforts to improve traffic safety in New York State have been successful. To hold fatalities at their present level in the face of low fuel prices, efforts must continue to enforce drinking and driving laws and to encourage citizens to wear the seat belt.

# 6

## *CALIFORNIA: HIGHWAY SAFETY IN THE LAND OF THE AUTOMOBILE*

✳

*IN NO U.S. STATE* does the automobile play a greater role than in California. Partially because of its size and extensive system of freeways and interstate highways, California led the nation in the total number of miles driven for the period of this study. Not surprisingly, because of the automobile's importance, drinking and driving has emerged as a significant concern of the California citizenry, and the state government has taken an innovative, if somewhat controversial, approach to address the problem. For these reasons, and the fact that California was one of the first to reform drinking and driving laws, California's experience is especially worthy of study.

The purpose of this chapter is to analyze the effects of two traffic safety reforms in California: the 1 January 1982 law that raised penalties and standardized punishments for drinking and driving; and the 1 January 1986 law mandating the use of seat belts. Compared to New York State and Michigan, California is similar to Great Britain in that it has not changed its minimum legal drinking age. But in contrast to the British legal drinking age of eighteen, California's legal drinking age has been maintained at twenty-one. In contrast to New York State, the California seat belt law includes only secondary enforcement: a driver must commit another offense or be involved in an accident in order to be cited for not wearing a seat belt.

The recent history of California's traffic safety reforms are reviewed and described below. Special attention is given to problems of implementing the DUI (driving under the influence) reform. Following the presentation of the methodology and data analysis, policy implications and theoretical relevance are discussed.

## *TRAFFIC SAFETY REFORM*

### *The DUI Reform: Background*

Compared to the debates in Great Britain, New York, and Michigan, the subject of drinking and driving in California was highly publicized. In fact, citizens partly led the battle against drinking and driving in California. The public interest group MADD (Mothers Against Drunk Driving) was founded in California in 1980 by Candy Lightner, whose thirteen-year-old daughter was killed by an intoxicated driver in May 1980.[1] Interest and membership in MADD spread rapidly through California, and chapters were soon founded in many other states.

Much credit must go to Lightner and her organization for changing attitudes and the law in California. Immediately after the death of her daughter, she had difficulty even getting an appointment with Governor Edmund Brown, Jr., to discuss legal reforms; but by the fall of 1980, she testified before Congress and persuaded Brown to establish California's Task Force on Alcohol, Drugs and Traffic Safety.[2] The task force realized quickly the extent of the drinking and driving problem. The *Los Angeles Times,* using statistics from the California Highway Patrol, estimated that 2,500 deaths and 73,000 injuries were caused annually by drunk drivers.[3] In Los Angeles County alone, there were 500 deaths and 21,000 injuries as a result of alcohol-related accidents.[4]

If the scope of the problem was wide, a more serious difficulty was the ineffectiveness of the criminal justice system to deal with the situation. Typically, punishments were light and plea bargaining was rampant. The most prominent plea bargain was the reduction of an alcohol-related traffic charge to reckless driving. The task force found that, of the 80,000 convictions for reckless driving in 1978, 75,000 of these motorists originally had been charged with DUI.[5] The situation in California was aptly summarized by Los Angeles City Attorney Burt Pines in testimony before the State Assembly Criminal Justice Committee. He said that although mandatory sentencing is common for crimes committed with a gun, "the drinking driver who threatens the lives of countless other people generally faces only a minimal fine of a few hundred dollars and summary probation."[6] The *Los Angeles Times* added the following comment in an editorial:

> There is a direct cause-and-effect relationship between the inadequacy of existing drunk-driving laws and the increasing slaughter on the state's highways and streets. We hope this will be the year the Legislature finally acknowledges this relationship.[7]

### *The DUI Reform: Passage of the Law*

As a result of the task force's work and hearings by the Criminal Justice Committee, a number of bills wound their way through the legislature during 1981. In the end, the package that was passed and signed by Governor Brown consisted of three primary pieces of legislation.

The first bill was introduced by Assemblyman Gary Hart.

It sets at 0.10 the minimum blood-alcohol concentration that categorizes a driver as driving under the influence. Up to the passage of this bill, a person driving with this concentration could argue that he or she was capable of driving.[8] The new law simply makes it illegal to drive at this concentration.

The second portion of the package deals with plea bargaining. It was introduced by Assemblyman Mel Levine. Most important, reckless driving convictions were henceforth counted as prior drunk-driving offenses if alcohol was involved. In addition, the legislation requires public explanation by judges and prosecutors in the event of plea bargaining.[9]

The third and most visible portion of the legislative package concerns minimum punishment for the DUI conviction.[10] Penalties were stiffened considerably. The bill was introduced by Assemblywoman Jean Moorhead. The most publicized aspect of the legislation is the mandatory jail sentence for the first offense. Specifically, the law calls for a two-day sentence but judges can substitute a ninety-day license suspension (except for driving to and from work). In addition, the first offender typically is fined from $375 to $500 and is required to attend an alcohol treatment program. A second offender receives ten days in jail, a maximum fine of $1,000, and has the license suspended for one year. Again, the suspension does not apply to work-related transportation or driving to an alcohol treatment program. In addition, by attending the one-year treatment program, the jail sentence can be reduced to two days. A reapplication for the license can be made in six months, and the driver can then have unrestricted driving privileges through the treatment program. However, an offender who fails the treatment program faces thirty days in jail and a one-year license suspension. Third offenders face license revocation, 120 days in jail, and a $5,000 fine. To address the problem of driving with a suspended license, a new penalty was added. First and second offenses carry the penalties of thirty and sixty days in jail, respectively.

The California law is complicated with detailed provisions.[11] Nevertheless, the publicity surrounding the law raises the perceived certainty and severity of punishment. When the law was under consideration, several horror stories emerged on the ineffectiveness of previous laws and the need for change. The most prominent example involves the conviction of the wealthy owner of a Los Angeles meat packing firm who was sentenced to four and a half years in the county jail for refusing to take a breath test.[12] This individual had nineteen drinking-related convictions dating back to 1959 and to this point had spent no time in jail. These offenses consisted of fifteen DUI convictions, three incidents of public drunkenness, and the current charge. Another important event that raised public consciousness on certainty and severity was the 16 September 1981 headline in the Los Angeles Times: ALL DRUNK DRIVERS TO BE JAILED.[13] Of course, the legislation was not written in this fashion, and comparatively few first offenders faced a jail term. Nevertheless, such publicity probably frightened many social drinkers.

### *The Mandatory Seat Belt Use Law*

The California legislative scene was relatively quiet during the next few years, chiefly because the state was not faced with the necessity of raising its minimum legal drinking age, as nearly all other states were. Beginning in 1985, discussion in the California legislature began on the desirability of mandatory seat belt use. The law that was passed, effective 1 January 1986, was weaker than the British or New York laws in that it allowed only secondary enforcement. It was necessary for another violation to occur for the motorist to receive a citation. The fine, much lower than in Great Britain and a bit lower than in New York State, is set at twenty dollars for a first offense and fifty dollars for each subsequent violation. Further, while some jurisdictions enforced the law immediately, the California Highway Patrol allowed a two-month warning period, issuing citations beginning on 1 March 1986.[14]

## *IMPLEMENTATION PROBLEMS*

Generally, compliance with seat belt laws in the United States is low. California is no exception. According to the University of North Carolina's Highway Safety Research Center, compliance rose from 18 to 47 percent immediately after the passage of the law, but did not increase after that point.[15] Still, compared to the DUI reform, implementation problems with the seat belt were mild. Law enforcement officials and the criminal justice system experienced difficulties with virtually every aspect of the new drinking and driving law.

Controversy first erupted over the 0.10 blood-alcohol provision when Ira Reiner, the new city attorney of Los Angeles, refused to prosecute under the drinking and driving reform.[16] Reiner argued that the 0.10 provision applied at the time of driving, and most breath or blood tests take place at a police station or hospital. A driver might have a drink just before driving, and in that case might have a blood-alcohol level of only 0.09 while driving, but the level could rise to 0.11 by the time a test took place in a police station. Thus the driver is not in violation of the law while driving. The opposite situation can occur, too—when the blood-alcohol level is illegal at the time of apprehension but falls below that level by the time of testing. To Reiner, this suggested the impractical necessity of calculating the blood-alcohol content when driving. While eventually the DUI law was found constitutional by the California Supreme Court, initial application without supplementary evidence in Los Angeles County was slow.

Other observers were fearful of the effect that the presumption of guilt at 0.10 concentration would have on the legal system. Attorney James E. Blatt thought it would discourage many people registering between the 0.10 and 0.13 level from plea bargaining.[17] He argued that attorneys with clients with this range of blood-alcohol concentration would advise them to plead not guilty and go to trial, which would cause a logjam in the courts and confusion in the criminal justice system. However, the new punishments are probably more responsible for crowding the courts than the legal blood-alcohol level. Because of a two-day jail term, fewer defendants enter guilty pleas, and there are significantly more demands for jury trials. Postponements of cases are more frequent, and guilty pleas are entered much later in the criminal justice process.[18]

For the most part, jail is avoided on the first offense, although the threat is always present. In Los Angeles County in 1982, 54,000 out of 56,000 first offenders received, in lieu of jail, the option of a fine, license restriction, probation, and a ninety-day alcohol education program.[19] Nevertheless, the jail option does raise some fundamental problems. For one, overcrowded jails throughout the state are ill equipped to manage several thousand more prisoners. A second difficulty is the concept of equal justice under the law for poor defendants. Although jail usually is avoided for the first offense, the driver must have a substantial amount of money to opt for probation and license restriction. The first-offender fine is $375, which does not include attorney fees and the possibility that automobile insurance premiums will be raised.

In addition, a ninety-day education program is part of the treatment, and first offenders must pay $200 and more to attend the course. As a consequence, poorer drivers choose the two-day jail sentence instead of license restriction. One jurist called the situation in Los Angeles County equivalent to a "debtor's prison."[20] Some members of the task force questioned the wisdom of charging any fee at all for the program. Many jurisdictions use the treatment program to make a profit for government, a practice that runs counter to the law's intent. However, if local government does not charge a fee, it raises the question as to how these programs should be financed. Presumably, the taxpayers would be asked to provide treatment funds for an unpopular group.

Other questions were raised about the treatment programs. For example, Orange County used offenders in experimental driving programs that involved alcohol use.[21] Offenders were given liquor and were told to negotiate a driving course; the purpose of the program was to measure the effect of alcohol on driving. Several members of the task force considered such "treatment" inappropriate, especially when so many convicted drunk drivers needed help to end their alcohol addiction.

In addition, many offenders escape prosecution or penalty by avoiding the law. For example, by the end of 1986 in Los Angeles County, over 100,000 bench warrants had been issued by judges to offenders who did not appear in court or pay their fines. A high proportion of these people were accused of alcohol-impaired driving under the new law.[22] Because of the large number of convictions under the DUI statute, and perhaps because drunk drivers are often transient, the marshall's office was not able to locate large numbers of offenders. Thus, while many pay the new penalties, basic accountability under the law has become a major problem in California. Reform has been proposed for the above mentioned problems, including a comprehensive information system to monitor the subsequent driving behavior of those convicted of DUI.[23]

Despite the above problems, a number of studies have found that in the short term the California legislative package has a deterrent effect.[24] For example, alcohol-related fatal accidents declined for twenty-one months after the implementation of the law, but with the primary effect in the second year.[25] In contrast, accidents unrelated to alcohol rose during this same period. Still unanswered is the law's longer term impact, combined with the seat belt intervention.

## RESEARCH DESIGN AND METHODOLOGY

Because California has not changed its minimum legal drinking age, the state presents a simpler model than New York. I analyze two interventions using the interrupted time series technique: the 1 January 1982 DUI reform and the 1 January 1986 seat belt law. The major methodological question is the precise time the seat belt law was put into effect. While the law was effective on the first day of the new year, the California Highway Patrol and many localities gave a two-month grace period. Yet the grace period was not uniform throughout the state. For example, the city of Glendale enforced the law with great vigor immediately with good publicity.[26] That municipality experienced a 12 percent decline in fatalities and injuries from the previous January. Compliance rose from 20 percent to 64 percent by the end of the month. According to the Highway Safety Research Center (HSRC), compliance in the state as a whole rose to 47 percent in January and stayed constant through March. Primarily for that reason, I used 1 January as the intervention point. But because the HSRC data are estimates provided by the individual states, I also experimented with 1 March as the date of the law's effect. I found no appreciable differences in the results. Other than these factors, the methodology was identical to that used for New York.

## ANALYSIS OF THE REFORMS

Despite the fact that there was a great deal of difficulty in enforcing and following the intent of the new DUI law, I still expected it would have an effect, mostly because of the considerable publicity it received. As the seat belt law used secondary enforcement, I was more doubtful of its impact. The first step in the data analysis was to examine the impact of the two interventions on the total number of fatalities from 1975 through 1987. These data are illustrated in figure 11 in the form of a twelve-month moving average.

Figure 11 suggests that through the end of 1980 there was a gradual increase in the number of automobile fatalities in California. This trend was modified somewhat by the end of that year to the beginning of 1981, perhaps because of publicity and discussion of the drunk driving problem. Another factor is the economic recession, which led to a lower number of miles driven in the state during this period. However, another shift in the series occurs in January 1982, the precise

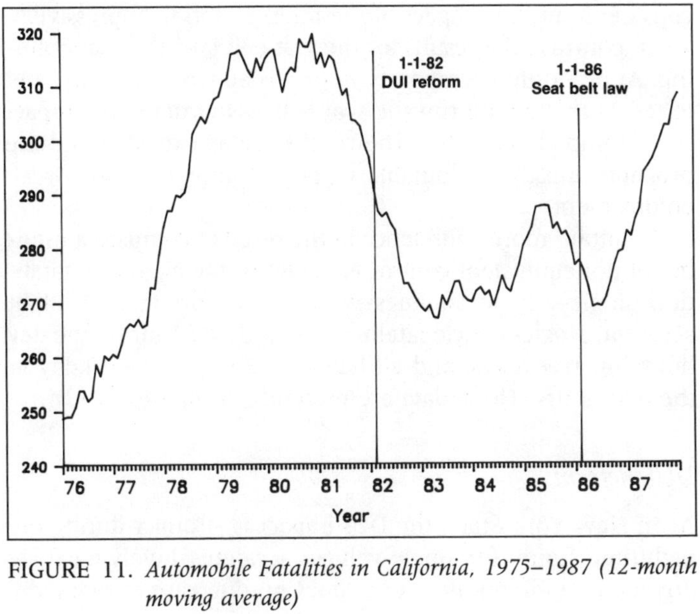


FIGURE 11. *Automobile Fatalities in California, 1975–1987 (12-month moving average)*

month when the DUI reform was effective. A low point also is reached following January 1986, the month of the effective date of the seat belt law; however, the data suggest that the change is temporary. Following the seat belt intervention, the series drifts upward, most likely because of increases in the number of miles driven and speed limit increases on rural interstates in California effective 29 May 1987. While the new minimum sixty-five-mile-per-hour speed limit applies only to rural interstates, there is evidence of spillover effects on many state roadways. This development is probably partially responsible for the casualty increase. Nevertheless, comparing the trend in deaths before and after the DUI intervention, there was an average decline of 28.49 fatalities per month beginning January 1982.[27] This translates to approximately a 10 percent decline. If the increase in number of miles driven is taken into consideration, the impact of the intervention is impressive.

In contrast, the results for the seat belt law are disappointing. At best only a temporary impact is apparent visually, and tested over the long run the seat belt has virtually no impact on automobile fatalities. The results are as expected and are probably mostly attributable to poor compliance and weak enforcement.

To attain more confidence in the results I compare a number of nonequivalent control variables to the aggregate fatalities: single-vehicle fatalities with a male driver in a night accident, single-vehicle fatalities for all drivers during the day hours on weekdays, and all fatalities during the weekday in the day hours. These data are presented in figures 12–14.

### *DUI Reform*

As in New York State, the DUI impact is stronger during the nighttime hours for single-vehicle accidents involving male drivers. In addition, this series does not increase as markedly

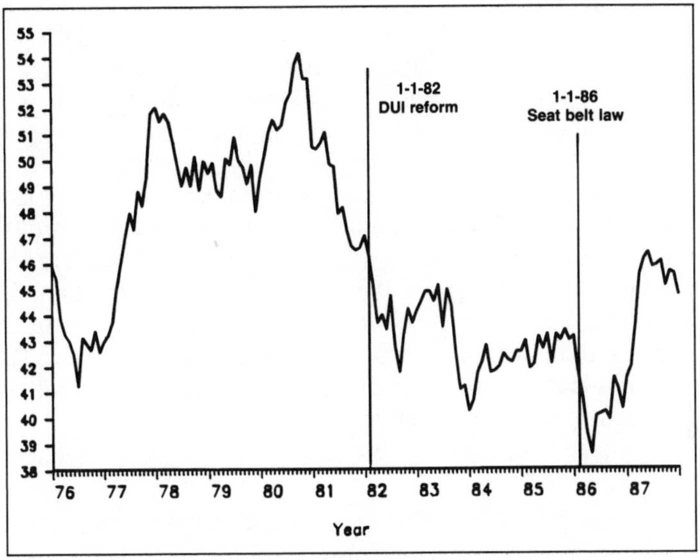


FIGURE 12. *Single-Vehicle Fatalities in California, Male Drivers, Nighttime, 1975–1987 (12-month moving average)*

during 1986 and 1987 as does the series in figure 11. The slighter increase gives additional support to the proposition that the law's effects are permanent despite the increase in the speed limit and the number of miles driven. If the impact of the 1982 law is fading, it would be more apparent in figure 12. Instead, the crashes more likely to involve alcohol maintain a lower level in the postintervention series compared to all fatalities. A comparison of preintervention and postintervention trend lines indicates an average savings of 10.37 lives per month, which translates to a postintervention series decline in fatalities of 21.5 percent. Thus, in accordance with expectation, the impact of the night series is much stronger than for all fatalities.

Somewhat surprising but consistent with the results in New York State is the impact of the seat belt law on the male driver, single-vehicle, nighttime fatalities. No doubt the mandatory use of seat belts may be an important factor in maintaining the lower level of fatalities for this series. If one takes into account the effects of the DUI reform, the seat belt legislation is responsible for a savings of approximately 4.56 additional lives per month for these drivers in the night hours (a 10 percent reduction). Again, the probable reason for the finding is that fatal and serious accidents are most likely to occur at night, and the seat belt is especially effective then.[28] Figure 12 indicates that the primary change in the nighttime fatalities occurred at the time of the interventions.

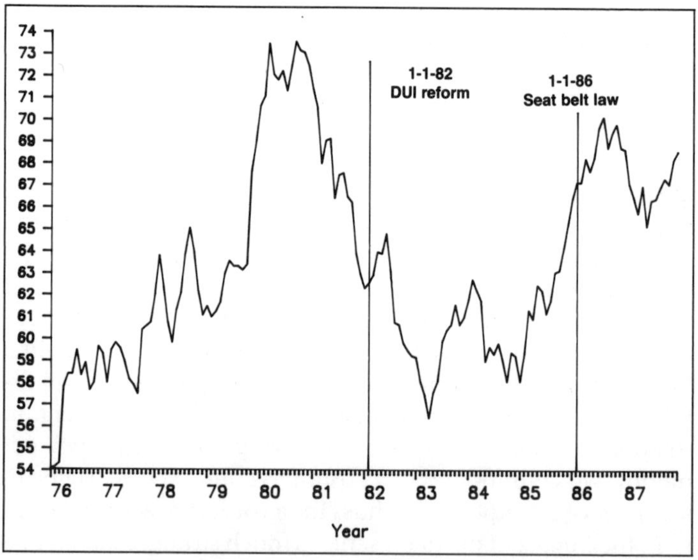


FIGURE 13. *Single-Vehicle Fatalities in California, All Drivers, Daytime, Weekdays, 1975–1987 (12-month moving average)*

Much flatter patterns are presented for single-vehicle fatalities occurring during the day (figure 13) and all daytime fatalities (figure 14). The single-vehicle, daytime, trend line rises immediately after the law's effective date and does not decline until several months into 1982. This is in contrast to the data shown in figures 11 and 12 and raises the question as to whether the decline is attributable to the intervention. For all daytime fatalities (figure 14), the trend line also rises after passage and changes even much less in later months. The weak results for the controls are confirmed in statistical tests, which show no effect for either the DUI or seat belt interventions.

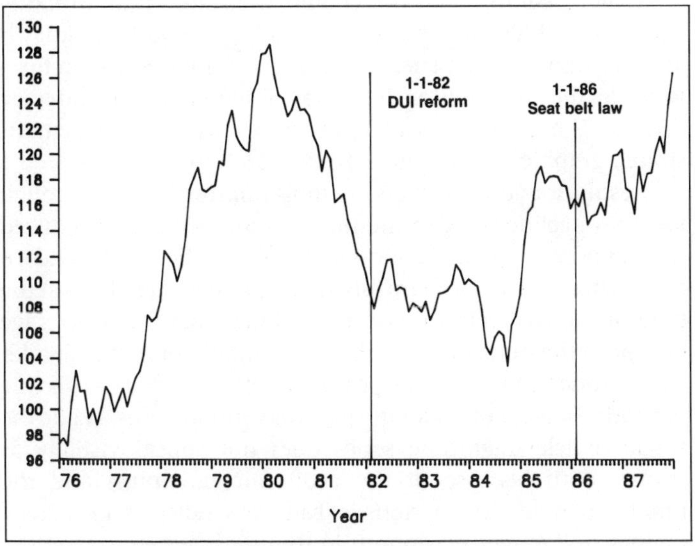


FIGURE 14. *Automobile Fatalities in California, All Drivers, Daytime, Weekdays, 1975–1987 (12-month moving average)*

## *The Seat Belt Law and Minimum Drinking-Age Law*

Thus far the seat belt intervention is shown to be ineffective for all fatality categories except for males involved in single-vehicle accidents at night. For the population as a whole, the intervention is weak. I illuminate the analysis of the seat belt law further by dividing occupants covered (front seat passengers) from those not covered. I hypothesize that if any effect were present it will occur for those riding in the front seat. I find an unimpressive reduction in fatalities of 3.1 percent in the postintervention series for front seat passengers. For other passengers, the seat belt produces virtually no effect. Again, the probable reason for the ineffectiveness of the law is its secondary enforcement provision. Results are consistent whether January or March is used as the onset month.

While California did not change the state's legal drinking age in the 1970s and 1980s, the number of youth fatalities is an important policy issue. Accordingly, I analyze DUI reform to see if the intervention has a favorable effect on underage drivers. The data for drivers under twenty-one are demonstrated graphically in figures 15 and 16.

Results for young drivers are most impressive. Even though fatalities decline prior to the intervention because of reduced driving occasioned by economic downturn, figures 15 and 16 demonstrate clearly a sharp fall in the number of fatalities at the time of the DUI reform. For all fatalities, there is an average decline in the trend line of 17 lives per month for persons under twenty-one throughout the postintervention period—a decline of nearly 14 percent under the preintervention series. While the single-vehicle, nighttime series does not appear visually as strong, both because of the economic downturn and the number of miles driven, statistical analysis indicates an average savings of 7.4 lives per month in the postintervention period. Disappointingly, the seat belt legislation does not lessen fatalities for younger drivers any more than for all motorists.

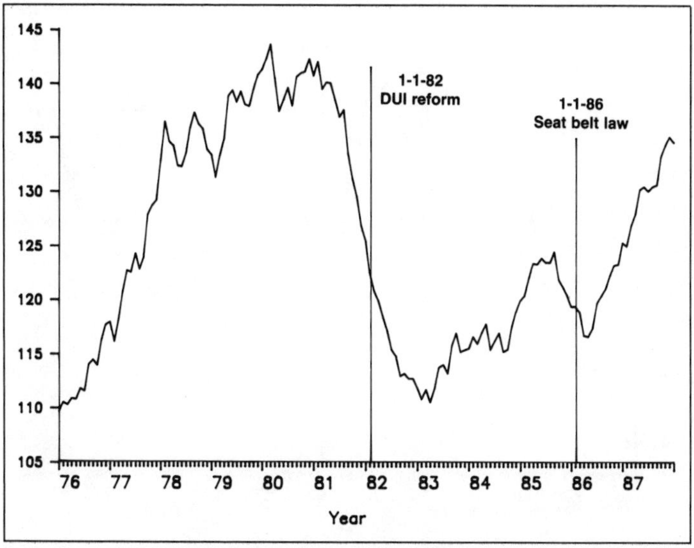


FIGURE 15. *Automobile Fatalities in California, Driver Under Age Twenty-one, 1975–1987 (12-month moving average)*

The policy implication of these findings is that a strong drinking and driving law has the potential to be a more effective deterrent to the young driver than a minimum drinking age. California maintained a legal drinking age of twenty-one through the period studied but still has a very severe problem with youth fatalities. The analysis indicates that, of the lives saved per month (twenty-eight), better than half involved drivers under age twenty-one. It also raises doubt that a higher legal drinking age should be the only strategy used by states to address this problem. Many young persons now driving were not exposed to the publicity and discussion of alcohol-impaired driving that took place earlier in the 1980s.[29] Despite the fact that all states now have a legal drinking age of twenty-one, drinking and driving by youths will not disappear. Analy-

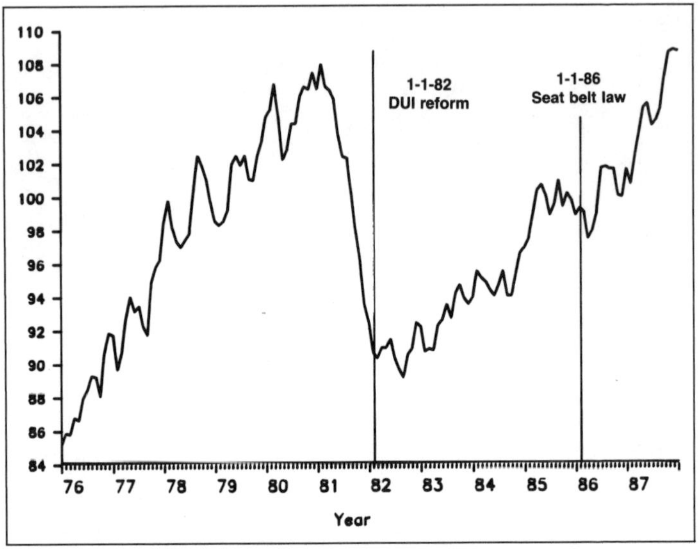


FIGURE 16. *Single-Vehicle Automobile Fatalities in California, Driver Under Age Twenty-one, Nighttime, 1975–1987 (12-month moving average)*

sis of California's youth fatalities indicates that the young will continue to obtain alcohol illegally and that they need other forms of deterrence to alter their behavior.

## *DISCUSSION*

The increase in the speed limit on rural interstate highways, effective 29 May 1987, is probably partly responsible for the rise in fatalities during the latter part of that year for nearly all series. At the very least, the higher speed limits enable motorists to cover more highway in a shorter period of time, raising the total number of miles driven and the subsequent risk of an accident. Too, there is the possibility of the higher speed limit on rural freeways having a spillover effect to other rural and urban roads. However, while some deterioration is evident, the number of lives saved per month is identical if the analysis is confined through 1986, with miles driven and economic conditions controlled.

The analysis of changes in California's law offers little support for the hypotheses presented in chapter 2. Mandatory seat belt use is hypothesized to be more easily acceptable to the citizenry, because wearing the belt does not involve dramatic alterations of habitual behavior. The literature suggests that at the very least the seat belt involves less individual sacrifice than not drinking before driving, behavior ingrained in the social patterns of the American population. Instead, I find the seat belt law to have little effect and the DUI reform to be a strong intervention.

In exploring the reasons for the effectiveness of the DUI law, one must be reasonably certain that it is the law itself that is responsible for the decline in fatalities. I have tried to eliminate rival hypotheses with nonequivalent dependent variables. Other evidence also is instructive. For example, enforcement of the new law is impressive. In 1980, 297,756 persons were arrested for driving under the influence of alcohol. By 1983 that number reached 342,203 and leveled at that approximate number during 1984 and 1985.[30] By 1986, DUI violations constituted 26 percent of all misdemeanor arrests in California. Clearly, there is little evidence of police being reluctant to arrest because of the more severe penalties of the 1982 law. Also, it is difficult to argue that fatalities dropped because of any changes in alcohol consumption. The amount of distilled spirits consumed in the state did drop very slightly in the early 1980s but not enough to explain the traffic fatality decline. California retained its rank as the state highest in the drinking of spirits, although, per capita, it ranks fourteenth, according to the latest available data. In addition, the lower consumption of spirits is offset by a rise in wine drinking through the early 1980s.

Even though the results of the California law seem impressive, I am reluctant to argue that traditional deterrence is at work—that increased punishment is responsible for altering behavior. The jail sentence, which received high publicity, is more a threat than a reality. It may not be the sanctions themselves that altered behavior but, rather, the public perception of punishment.[31] In short, people perceive that they will be punished more severely under the law, raising the seeming certainty of punishment, even though the actual consequences are in most cases only slightly more severe than the situation before passage of the law. I am persuaded by this argument and believe that the California law is successful because it adds an element of certainty (although perhaps not celerity) of punishment to the traditional notion of deterrence. Continued public interest in the issue has also helped make the effect of the law more permanent. In addition to a heightened awareness, Californians have grown averse to drinking and driving compared to their attitudes before the 1980s. Groups such as MADD deserve credit for helping to change these attitudes.

California also illustrates that policy makers cannot turn their backs on the problem of alcohol-impaired driving by young persons, even though the drinking age is now twenty-one in all states. In addition to passing minimum drinking-age laws, officials must be certain that drinking and driving laws be strictly enforced and targeted toward young persons, the group most vulnerable to the tragedies on highways. In addition to reforms such as the California DUI law, efforts to increase alcohol awareness among young drivers should be encouraged. An example is the Georgia law that requires a driver to pass an alcohol education program to obtain a license at age sixteen. The classic killer drunk is not primarily responsible for the wreckage on the nation's highways; California illustrates that drinking and driving is a pervasive problem among very young drivers. Creative efforts must be made to address this issue apart from mandating a legal drinking age.

The California experience also suggests that in and of itself a legal drinking age of twenty-one does not prevent fatalities, especially when the age has been maintained for a long time. Rather, it is raising the legal age that improves policy effects. To examine this proposition fully, we next examine the Michigan experience.

# 7

## *MICHIGAN: RAISING THE DRINKING AGE AND DETERRENCE THROUGH CERTAINTY*

✳

IN *NEW YORK* and California, the initial effort to improve traffic safety focused on the alcohol-impaired driver. In contrast, the state of Michigan is unique in that its primary policy focused on the problem of underage drinking and its tragic consequences on the highway. While most states did not become concerned with the minimum legal drinking age until federal and citizen pressure forced it to in the early to mid-1980s, Michigan took action much earlier. Specifically, a November 1978 citizen referendum raised the drinking age from eighteen to twenty-one effective on December 23 of that year. Thus, Michigan represents a more sweeping approach to raising the drinking age, as contrasted to the incremental policy in New York and nearly all other states.

I replicate the analysis of a 1984 study,[1] using a different dependent variable, the traffic fatality. I examine the effects of the 1978 law along with the 1983 reform of drinking and driving laws and the 1985 seat belt law. The 1983 law is important in terms of deterrence theory, because it provides for certainty of punishment, as opposed to severity. Existing fines and jail terms were kept, but the probability of losing the driver's license, at least temporarily, was much higher. Finally, the 1985 seat belt law provides another chance to view the effects of a secondary enforcement law. As in past chapters, I begin with a historical discussion of the legislation, describe the methodology, move into the data analysis, and then discuss the theoretical and policy implications.

## *TRAFFIC SAFETY REFORM*

### *Raising the Drinking Age: Background*

With the 30 June 1971 ratification of the Twenty-sixth Amendment to the Constitution giving eighteen-year-olds the right to vote, Michigan joined most other states in lowering the legal drinking age: in January 1972, the legal age was lowered from twenty-one to eighteen for all alcoholic beverages. Without much thought for the safety consequences, most legislators and citizens reasoned that if eighteen-year-olds were adults in other areas of civic obligation (such as military conscription and voting), they should be considered adults in alcohol consumption. Also, many argued that underage drinking was impossible to stop. By closing taverns and other public drinking places to young persons, youthful drinking would continue to occur in automobiles. Also, if adjacent states had lower drinking ages, it may cause some young people to travel to these states to consume alcohol, which could result in higher injuries and fatalities on the highway for both the young driver and others.

While these hypotheses no doubt were accurate, as the 1970s progressed, Michigan policy makers began to be more concerned with high fatalities and injuries among young drivers within the state. A 1977 study finds that the lowered drinking age of January 1972 was associated with increased crash involvement for young drivers, an increase ranging between 17 and 35 percent, depending upon the age group.[2]

A referendum, known as Proposition D, proposed that the drinking age be raised to twenty-one effective ten days after election results were certified (23 December 1978). The referendum originated with the Michigan Council on Alcohol Problems, which collected more than 317,000 signatures on petitions by September 1978.[3] It should be stressed that the council's position was not taken exclusively or even primarily because of concern over automobile casualties among the young; rather, general concern over alcohol abuse seemed to spur interest in thc referendum.

The change was not popular among those people most affected, and the legislature was not eager to deal with the issue directly. Partially in an effort to forestall Proposition D, the legislature passed a law earlier in 1978 raising the drinking age from eighteen to nineteen, effective 3 December 1978. In addition, the legislature reduced penalties then in effect for underage drinking.[4] Specifically, underage drinking no longer was a criminal offense with a possible fine of $500 and a maximum six months in jail. Instead, a person violating the legal drinking age faced a civil penalty, with a $25 fine for the first offense and $50 and $100 for second and third violations, respectively. The strategy was not deterrence but stressed the health benefits of not drinking.

As election day neared, considerable opposition was manifested toward Proposition D. Bar and restaurant owners formed the Michigan Committee for Age Responsibility (MICAR). The committee's specific interest was the proposition's potential economic impact on business. The group's slogan was STOP PROHIBITION, and some bars had voter registration booths on their premises to encourage people to register their opposition to the referendum.[5] In the 1970s Michigan was facing severe economic problems, with lower automobile sales. Thus, the issue of jobs was especially sensitive. One spokesman for MICAR estimated that the new law could cost approximately 10,000 service jobs in the restaurant-beverage industry and 5,000 positions for musicians.[6] In the end, MICAR spent approximately $170,000 in a public relations campaign to defeat Proposition D.[7]

Also, MICAR was instrumental in mobilizing another and perhaps more vocal opposition group—people between the ages of eighteen and twenty who would lose their drinking privileges. Prior to the election, one professional statewide poll found that 77 percent of the population favored Proposition D.[8] Interestingly, 71 percent of those who recently had achieved majority age (twenty-two- to twenty-five-year-olds) also favored raising the drinking age. In contrast, 58 percent of those aged eighteen to twenty-one were opposed. In Ann Arbor and East Lansing, homes of the University of Michigan and Michigan State University, respectively, voter registration rose dramatically, presumably because of opposition to Proposition D.[9] The typical reaction of college-age students was best expressed by Chris Mangus, then a freshman at Michigan State and a spokesperson for a student advocacy group known as the Three O'Clock Lobby.

> There's no way the new law can be enforced for 47,000 college students [at MSU]. They've had the right to drink for a number of years and all of a sudden you expect them to stop with the wave of a magic wand. There will be more drinking going on in dorms, cars, and other places. The new drinking environment will probably be more dangerous than the old one.[10]

Despite the protests of students and the restaurant industry, Proposition D easily passed with a 58 percent majority. It took effect on 23 December 1978.

## *Raising the Drinking Age: Legal Action*

The most important contribution of MICAR to the student protest was that it supported eighteen-, nineteen-, and twenty-year-olds in a class action suit against the state. The plaintiffs' chief point was that Proposition D violated the equal protection clause of the Fourteenth Amendment to the Constitution.[11] More specifically, the suit contended that the amendment

- seeks to establish two distinct classes of adults, those under age twenty-one and those over, who would be treated differently—which is illegal under the equal protection clause in the Fourteenth Amendment;
- prohibits any person under age twenty-one using an alcoholic beverage for any purpose, including sacramental purposes—a violation of Michigan law guaranteeing freedom of religion;
- threatens property losses to adults under age twenty-one who hold liquor licenses, and to those employees and barkeepers who would suddenly become underaged.[12]

While the plaintiffs hired a prestigious legal firm to handle the case, Ralph Guy, Jr., the federal judge in U.S. District Court in Detroit, held that the new amendment was constitutional. In a fifty-two-page opinion, the judge "cited the broad rights of states in making liquor regulations."[13] He also seemed persuaded by the testimony of state officials, who cited "dramatic increased drinking-related accidents and fatalities occurring since the drinking age was lowered to eighteen."[14] Finally, Guy held that the right of the voter to pass amendments to the state constitution in referenda was important and that such decisions should be upheld if there is a rational basis to support public action. The judge believed that the state provided such a rational basis by presenting evidence on the negative effect of lowering the drinking age in 1972. Thus, the new law took effect on the day of Guy's decision, 23 December 1978.

## *Raising the Drinking Age: Implementation*

As we have seen so often throughout this volume, the effectiveness of a law is only as good as the level of enforcement and the care in its implementation. For this law, numerous problems were evident. To begin, some police were loath to enforce the law, feeling that other problems were more important. Lowell Henline, president of the Michigan Association of Chiefs of Police, stated that officers had "mixed emotions" about enforcement and, while he indicated that police had not "turned their backs on it," they were "not shaking the bushes on it either."[15] Further, the state decriminalized underage drinking, making it a civil offense. Finally, two university towns, Ann Arbor and East Lansing opted for five-dollar fines. The penalty for underage drinking in Ann Arbor is similar to that city's decriminalization of marijuana use in small amounts. Some contend that the lower penalties caused the police to lose interest in enforcement.[16]

At least in the short run, the economic impact on bars was severe. Many taverns, especially in university areas, were on the brink of closing immediately after the effective date of the referendum. One strategy used by the bars was "double stamping."[17] Underage patrons were admitted to taverns, their hands were stamped, but they were not served alcohol; those who were of legal age received a different stamp, indicating eligibility for alcohol consumption. In the long run, some evidence indicates that the bars broadened their appeal to older drinkers by offering different types of music and entertainment.

Another short-term adjustment by bar owners was to ignore the law. Apparently this practice was widespread. The *Detroit Free Press* sent an underage employee to sixteen bars and restaurants in the Detroit area shortly after the effective date of the new law; only two of the sixteen refused to serve alcohol to the young woman.[18] They disobeyed the law even though they could have their liquor license suspended if a bartender did not make a "diligent" effort to determine the age of a patron. Further, an underage patron who used a false identification to buy alcohol would have committed a misdemeanor, while only a civil penalty would be incurred by mere possession or drinking.

The weak enforcement of the amendment may raise questions about its effectiveness, yet alcohol-related casualties were significantly reduced through 1984. It is my purpose to explore the law's impact on fatalities in competition with the 30 March 1983 drinking and driving reform and the 1 July 1985 seat belt law.

### *Drinking and Driving Laws: Background*

Compared to New York and California, Michigan was relatively slow in reforming laws related to the alcohol-impaired driver. Initial proposals were discussed in the Michigan legislature early in 1982. With the sponsorship of the Mothers Against Drunk Driving (MADD), State Senator Steven V. Mansma offered legislation that might best be described as traditional deterrence; increasing the punishment for the alcohol-impaired driver would supposedly alter behavior.[19] Specifically, the Mansma bills called for higher fines and two-day jail sentences for a first offense.

The Mansma bills were amended gradually, and the bill that eventually was signed into law by Governor William Milleken is unique. Anyone convicted of operating a motor vehicle while impaired by alcohol loses the driver's license for a minimum of ninety days on the first offense. Prior to the new law, the license was suspended, but the duration of suspension was left to the sentencing judge. In some jurisdictions, such as Kent County (Grand Rapids), licenses already were suspended for ninety days, but in most areas of the state, the 1983 law meant a longer term of punishment.[20] In addition, before the 1983 law, motorists charged with operating under the influence (OUI—legally, a blood-alcohol concentration of .010 or greater) could plead guilty to the lesser offense of operating while impaired (OWI—legally, a blood-alcohol concentration between 0.07 and 0.099) and retain the license. The new law means that the license is suspended with an alcohol concentration of .07 or greater.

Penalties become more severe as offenses and alcohol concentration increase. For example, a first offense of OWI requires a ninety-day to one-year suspension, a second infraction a six- to eighteen-month suspension, and a third violation a one-year minimum revocation of the license. Prior to the 1983 reform, a driver could commit three OWI violations and retain the license. For OUI, a first offense results in a six-month to two-year suspension, a one-year minimum suspension for the second offense, and a five-year minimum suspension for the third infraction. For both OWI and OUI infractions, fines at the approximate level of previous years were imposed. Although they varied widely throughout the state, the average fine levied for the convicted driver was $366 in 1983.[21] It should be kept in mind that since this figure is for all drivers, the average for the first offender is lower.

### *Drinking and Driving Laws: Enforcement and Implementation*

In terms of enforcement, the 1983 law contains a per se provision, much like California's, which states that a 0.10 blood-alcohol concentration is a violation in and of itself. Up to this point, the blood-alcohol concentration was only one piece of evidence used in drunk-driving cases. Also, for the first time, police are able to use curbside breath tests to measure blood-alcohol content; up to 30 March 1983, most testing was conducted in police stations. In addition, judges can impose a fine of $100 for refusing the test. The new law also contains treatment provisions: each convicted driver is assessed for need of alcohol education and counseling. Finally, the new legislation mandates the Michigan Department of State Police to compile an annual report on drinking and driving.

Predictably, the new legislation brings with it enforcement and implementation problems. One immediate problem is curbside breath testing: the equipment is expensive, approximately $400 per unit, and many police departments simply cannot afford the device.[22] This leaves open the possibility that the concentration could fall below the legal limit by the time a driver is transported to the police station for testing. A second and possibly more serious problem is that the reform does not eliminate plea bargaining. Many prosecutors continue to accept a plea for OWI even for drivers operating at 0.10 or greater. An apparent reason for accepting the lesser plea is that many prosecutors and judges do not wish to overcrowd the courts with drunk-driving cases.[23] It is important to note that an acceptance of the lesser plea no longer permits the driver to escape license suspension; however, it does shorten the length of this penalty considerably. In addition, immediately after the law was passed some counties did not fully follow its intent. Specifically, restricted licenses were given in lieu of full punishment.

Despite such problems, the police appear to have enforced the law vigorously. People arrested for OUI rose to 65,451 in 1983, from 53,111 arrests in 1982.[24] The number arrested in 1984 increased to 79,812, a gain of 21.9 percent over the previous year. Also, the initial results appear positive: the number of drinking drivers involved in fatal accidents declined by about 12 percent in 1983. This drop occurred in spite of an increased number of miles driven yearly by Michigan motorists. However, we cannot be certain of the law's impact on fatalities without using more sensitive monthly data and considering reforms in the minimum drinking age and the seat belt law.

### *The Seat Belt Law*

Traffic deaths in Michigan rose for the first time in six years in 1984.[25] Many observers believe that the low number of traffic deaths in 1983 (1,294) was due to the reforms in drinking and driving legislation, so the 1,508 deaths reported in 1984 was disappointing. One possible explanation is that the new drunk-driving legislation had its usual short-term impact. However, other observers believe that not using a seat belt was responsible: 93 percent of the persons killed in traffic accidents in Michigan in 1984 did not wear a seat belt, and police estimate usage at 18 percent.[26]

The seat belt not only is a safety issue in the state, but also an economic issue. The U.S. Department of Transportation requires air bags in American cars unless three-quarters of the states mandate seat belt use. Car manufacturers estimate that the air bags will add $1,000 to the price of a new car.[27] Ironically, the Michigan seat belt law does not meet the federal government's minimum standards: it does not include primary enforcement and initially had a fine of less than twenty-five dollars for a first offense. In addition, the law provides that the law would be voided, effective 1 April 1989, if the federal government mandated air bags. However, the law continues to the present day.

Passage of a seat belt law did not come easily in Michigan. As in other states, many motorists and some public officials were skeptical of the belt's efficacy and resented what they considered unwarranted federal interference. In December 1984, the state House fell four votes short of approving a Senate-passed bill for front seat belts.[28] Several of the lawmakers who opposed the 1984 legislation were defeated in the November elections, and this eased passage of the law in

March 1985. The law provides for secondary enforcement and a ten-dollar fine for a first offense. The fine rose to twenty-five dollars, effective 1 January 1986; however, secondary enforcement did not change. The first effective day of the law was 1 July 1985.

The new seat belt law received a great deal of publicity. Public service advertisements appeared on television featuring such personalities as Jud Heathcote, Michigan State University basketball coach.[29] The Michigan Office of Highway Safety provided a toll-free number so the public could ask questions about the new law. Some supporters were wildly optimistic, claiming that mandatory use of seat belts could save 300 lives and $200 million per year in wages, health care costs, and other expenses from traffic accidents.[30] State police were supportive, although indications were they would "go easy" at first.[31] The public also was positive, at least if one believes opinion surveys taken. One poll found 67 percent of the citizens in favor of the new law (71 percent in Detroit); only 5 percent said they never would comply.[32]

The literature of survey research reveals that actual behavior often is at variance with answers provided to an interviewer, especially when socially desirable behavior is involved. The degree of compliance with the seat belt law varies depending on which traffic survey one accepts, but all agree that it is below the report of citizen surveys. A direct observation survey by the University of Michigan Transportation Research Institute (UMTRI) finds a pattern similar to New York's.[33] Prelaw use in Michigan was around 20 percent and rose to nearly 60 percent after passage in July. But following the law's effective date, compliance declined and leveled off in the mid-40 percent range. Interestingly, seat belt use increased prior to passage, probably due to the publicity surrounding the law. A survey by the *Detroit Free Press* suggested slightly higher compliance immediately after 1 July 1985: statewide, compliance was around 65 percent; in

Detroit, compliance was 58 percent.[34] However, the survey does not cover subsequent periods, and it observed drivers only at ten of Michigan's most dangerous intersections. Only 100 observations were made in Detroit. It could be that drivers' knowledge of danger at some intersections made seat belt use more likely. By the year's end, positive responses dropped even in telephone surveys, with fewer than 60 percent of one sample saying they buckled up "all the time."[35] The falloff in positive responses is confirmed by the UMTRI data, which indicate a lower usage rate by this time.[36]

## *RESEARCH DESIGN AND METHODOLOGY*

Three Michigan interventions are analyzed: the 23 December 1978 drinking-age change from eighteen to twenty-one, the 30 March 1983 law regarding alcohol-impaired driving, and the 1 July 1985 seat belt law. For the drinking-age change and the drinking and driving reform, 1 January 1979 and 1 April 1983 were used as the onset dates.

An issue of concern for the seat belt law was the fine increase from ten dollars to twenty-five on 1 January 1986. News reports and the available literature give no indication that compliance was any higher at this time than previously, and some evidence indicates that enthusiasm was waning.[37] At best, a temporary effect was apparent visually, but this is contradicted by the literature, which suggests that the benefits of seat belt laws are permanent. Accordingly, I use July 1985 as the first intervention month.

I began with the assumption that the Michigan drinking and driving reform had temporary effects, just as in New York and California. After examining a number of alternative models, I realized that the new law has a more permanent impact.

## *ANALYSIS OF THE REFORMS*

I first examined the impact of the interventions on the entire population of fatalities (see figure 17). The trend line makes it clear that a dramatic shift in the series occurs immediately following the effective date of the drinking-age reform. This finding is in contrast to expectation, for in New York State, I was unable to find consistent impacts even for targeted age groups. A statistical analysis of the preintervention and post-intervention trend lines indicates that since January 1979 the drinking-age law saved an average of almost twelve lives per month. (The tests of the intervention effects are avail-

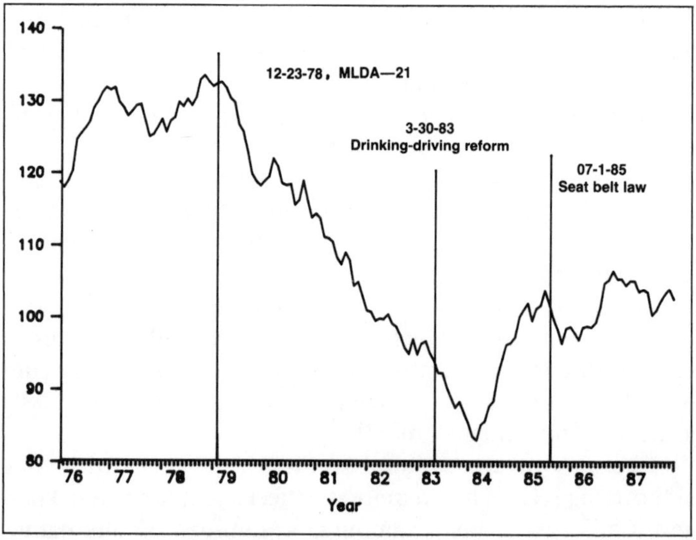


FIGURE 17. *Automobile Fatalities in Michigan, 1975–1987 (12-month moving average)*

able in Appendix 1). The monthly figure translates to an average of over 140 lives per year and approximately 1,260 lives through 1987. This is apart from the effects of the other interventions.[38]

There are a few plausible explanations for the surprising finding. Most important, raising the drinking age was the first step taken by Michigan to improve highway safety. While the law may not have been written explicitly for that purpose, it was a first intervention, and went into effect several years before drinking and driving was a "hot" policy issue for the American public. Just as drinking and driving reform lowered fatalities in New York and California and the seat belt lowered them in Great Britain, the drinking-age law was the trigger of traffic safety reform in Michigan. A second explanation for the law's general effect may be that young drivers killed and injured not only themselves but also other drivers. Indeed, the drinking-age law affected both single-vehicle and multiple-vehicle accidents. A primary effect is evident on young male drivers in single vehicles at night; in addition, my analysis indicates a spillover effect for all drivers.[39]

Figure 17 indicates that the trend line continues to decline following the 30 March 1983 reform of drinking and driving laws. But it is impossible to determine whether the reform triggered an independent effect or if the additional reduction is a product of the continued benefit of the drinking-age law. A statistical analysis of the trend line following the drinking-driving reform indicates a permanent and significant decline in the postintervention series independent of the effects of the drinking-age law, the economy, or the number of miles driven. Approximately fifteen lives per month were saved from the time of intervention through 1987, a decline of 12.7 percent. To confirm the law's effectiveness, I again use some series of nonequivalent control. Data are presented in figures 18–20.

Although there are fewer observations of fatalities for

single-vehicle accidents involving male drivers at night, the drop in the trend line is more pronounced than is the case for all fatalities (figure 18). Statistical analysis indicates an average savings of four lives per month for the drinking-age reform, a fatality decline of almost 21 percent. In contrast, figures 19 (single-vehicle daytime fatalities) and 20 (all daytime fatal accidents) show smaller reductions, although there is a significant difference between the preintervention and postintervention series for single-vehicle daytime accidents.

Although I did not expect this finding in the original hypotheses, results are identical to those in New York. This raises the methodological question as to whether single-vehicle acci-

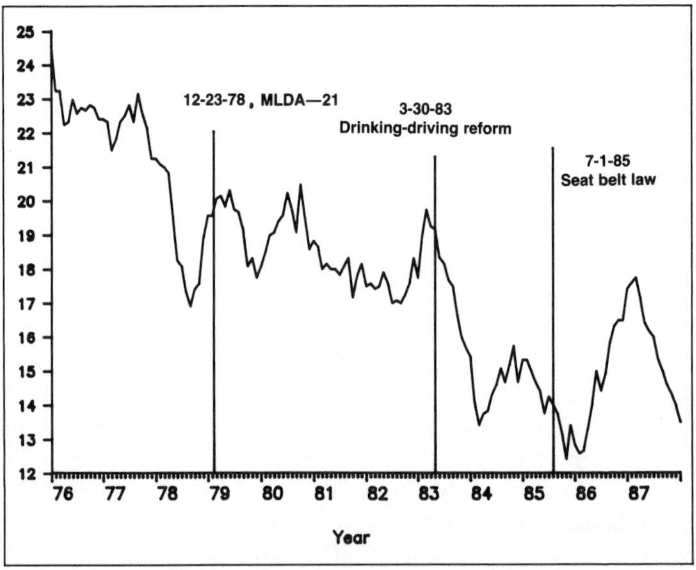


FIGURE 18. *Single-Vehicle Fatalities in Michigan, Male Drivers, Nighttime, 1975–1987 (12-month moving average)*

dents during the day can be used as a control against night crashes. Perhaps efficacious traffic safety policies uniformly affect all single-vehicle accidents. Also, it is possible that the amount of drinking and driving that occurs during the day is underestimated or that nighttime drinking and driving is exaggerated. In short, considerable measurement error probably exists in both indicators. In line with expectation, the effect of the reform is not significant for all drivers involved in fatal accidents during the day (figure 20). Although the impact of the intervention is in the correct direction, fatalities among this group are better explained by the deteriorating condition of the Michigan economy.

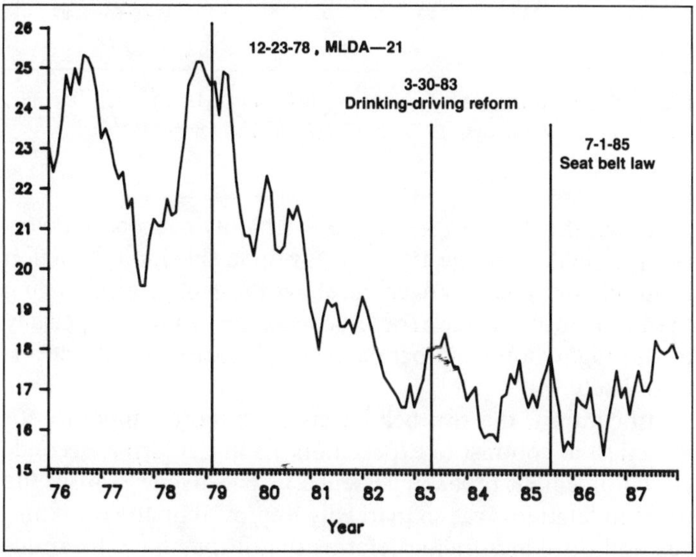


FIGURE 19. *Single-Vehicle Fatalities in Michigan, All Drivers, Daytime, Weekdays, 1975–1987 (12-month moving average)*

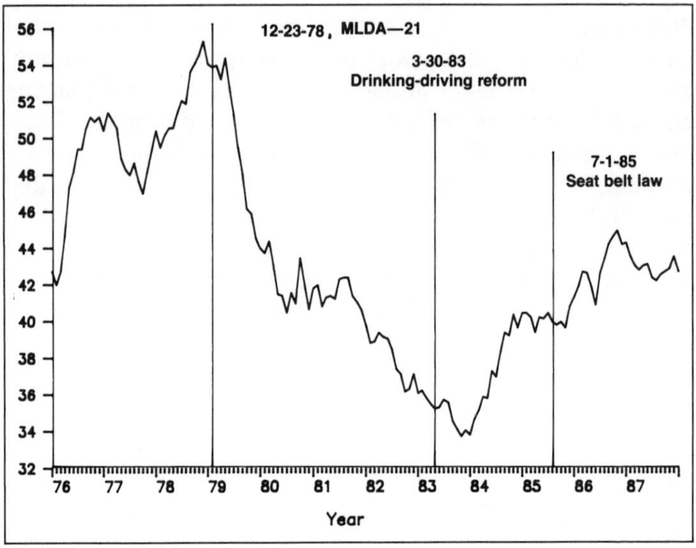


FIGURE 20. *Automobile Fatalities in Michigan, All Drivers, Daytime, Weekdays, 1975–1987 (12-month moving average)*

In all, the data suggest that the certainty concept of deterrence embedded in the 1983 law is responsible for a reduction in automobile fatalities over and above the gains from changing the legal drinking age. These benefits are realized especially in the night hours—a period when drinking and driving is most likely.

In contrast, the seat belt effects seem more temporary for all series, in contrast to expectation. As in California, secondary enforcement probably lessened its effectiveness. Also, the trend in fatalities was so markedly improved by the drinking-age and drinking-driving reforms that it may have been difficult to effect further change in the trend line. The lack of impact may be explained more fully by the fact that the number of miles driven by the Michigan motorist also was increasing throughout this period. However, before dismissing the law as ineffective, I examine its impact in more detail below and explore the drinking-age change among affected groups.

### *Seat Belt and Drinking-Age Laws*

To examine the impact of mandatory seat belt use more fully, I separated front seat passengers from those occupying back seats. Since the law applies only to drivers and front seat passengers, I expected that if there is any impact, it will be felt primarily among those in the front seat. Statistical analysis reveals that the law impacted neither group. Further, because data from the UMTRI indicate that increased compliance occurred as early as April 1985, I tested for the possibility that benefits are evident beginning then, but this hypothesis is not confirmed.[40] Also, the seat belt law is weak compared to strength of the drinking-age and drinking-driving reforms for both sets of passengers.

More interesting data are presented in figures 21 and 22. Figure 21, which illustrates traffic fatalities for drivers under twenty-one years of age, is similar to figure 17 (fatalities for all ages). Statistical analysis of the trend line indicates that the intervention is significant and is responsible for a savings of approximately nine fatalities per month in this age category. This figure is equivalent to a postintervention series decline of nearly 15 percent over and above other interventions. Figure 22, which details fatalities for single-vehicle drivers under age twenty-one, is a mirror of figure 21, and analysis indicates that the drinking-age law was effective for the accident involving a single vehicle and an underage driver. Such accidents are more likely to involve alcohol than multiple-vehicle crashes. These effects occurred despite the rise in number of miles driven in the state which greatly increases the risk of accident.

Another interesting point apparent visually and confirmed

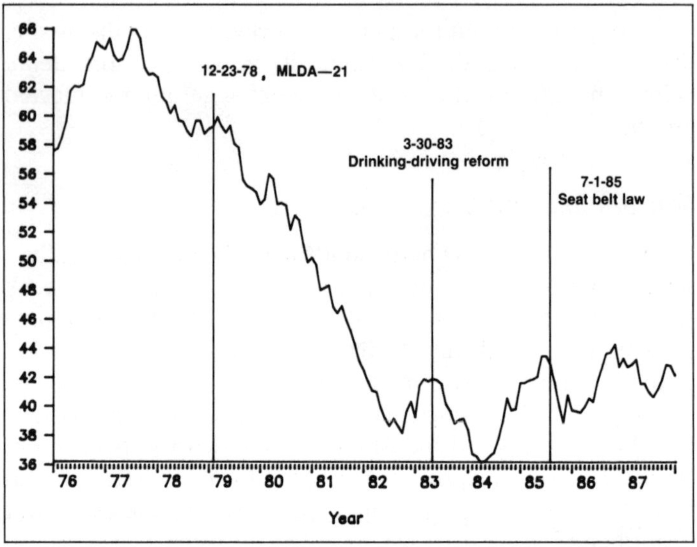


FIGURE 21. *Automobile Fatalities in Michigan, Driver Under Age Twenty-one, 1975–1987 (12-month moving average)*

by statistical analysis is that the changes in the drinking-driving law in 1983 also had a favorable effect on young drivers. In this sense, the evidence in Michigan parallels the California data and has the important policy implication that a high drinking age does not ensure the greatest possible reduction of deaths to young motorists. For underage drivers, the drinking-driving reform is responsible for saving almost the same number of lives as the drinking-age change.[41] These findings are especially impressive in that the estimates presented in table A-14 (in the appendix) indicate that the unemployment rate tends to depress fatalities for young drivers.

Finally, those who find reductions in deaths for citizens under age twenty-one sometimes ignore the potentially harm-

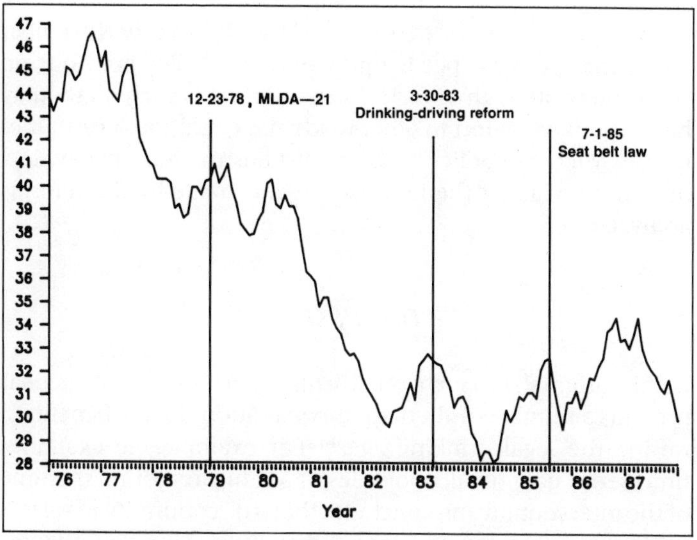


FIGURE 22. *Single-Vehicle Automobile Fatalities in Michigan, Driver Under Age Twenty-one, 1975–1987 (12-month moving average)*

ful effects on twenty-one-year-olds of raising the drinking age.[42] Those who oppose a higher drinking age argue that the attainment of majority age, not the age itself, is responsible for greater highway casualties. Separate analysis indicates that although there is a deleterious effect of the drinking age on this group, it is weak and insignificant. Not only is the drinking-age change not harmful to this group, but also the insignificance of the coefficient increases confidence that the legal age had a strong effect on the targeted groups.

While New York and California demonstrate increased fatalities beginning in 1986 and continuing through 1987, Michigan shows slighter evidence of such a trend. This is especially encouraging, because more miles were driven during these years. The continued safety of the Michigan motorist may be in jeopardy with the passage of a law, effective 29 November 1987, that permits speeds up to sixty-five miles per hour on rural interstate highways.[43] As in California, such a law may have a spillover effect to other roads and could cause casualties to rise. Michigan policy makers must ensure that the new law does not endanger the impressive gains made by the reforms analyzed here.

## *DISCUSSION*

In his original research on Michigan, Alexander Wagenaar presents a number of alternative explanations for the benefits of raising the legal drinking age.[44] For example, he examines time-series data on alcohol sales in Michigan around the time of the intervention and concludes that a discontinuity in sales is not responsible for the lower casualties. Nor can the reductions be attributed to the deposit on bottled and canned alcoholic beverages instituted at that time. There was some reduction in the drinking of draft beer—the beverage most likely for young drinkers to consume. Of course, most draft beer is sold in taverns, which banned young drinkers effective 23 December 1978. On the basis of Wagenaar's analysis and the present study, one can have little doubt that the drinking-age change in Michigan was beneficial not only to young drivers but also to the entire population of motorists.

The results for Michigan conflict with those for New York regarding the raising of the drinking age. A number of reasons explain the contradictory findings. In New York, drinking-age changes were preceded by a strong drinking and driving reform, which drove fatalities downward. It may be that further improvement in the data became difficult or that the statistical analysis could not detect significant effects for such a small number of cases. A second explanation for the contradictory findings is that the law in Michigan became effective relatively early and was more sweeping than in New York. By the time New York raised its drinking age from nineteen to twenty-one on 1 December 1985, many other inducements to safety already had occurred, including a seat belt law with primary enforcement. Finally, curfew and age-licensing restrictions are not in force in Michigan, in contrast to New York. Perhaps the Michigan law demonstrates a stronger effect because a greater proportion of young persons were driving in 1978.

In terms of drinking-driving legislation, the Michigan experience is instructive especially with regard to the importance of the certainty of punishment. The possibility of plea bargaining remains in the Michigan law, and many take advantage of it. Evidently, many prosecutors and judges are willing to trade severity for celerity, and Michigan has not had the court logjam that California has. Also, traditional deterrence is somewhat supported in that punishment is increased for those driving while alcohol-impaired (the lesser of the alcohol-related violations). However, the key deterrent factor of the law is that the driver's license is suspended with a 0.07 blood-alcohol level. The results for Michigan are similar to California's except that while in California certainty is increased primarily by the *threat* of jail, the Michigan law works because the motorist is sure that the driver's license will be suspended. Even short periods of suspension may be a more effective deterrent than fines or jail terms for first offenders.[45] Also, the Michigan experience supports the California findings regarding the effect of strong drinking-driving laws on young drivers. Youth fatalities were significantly reduced beyond the reductions attributable to drinking-age reform.

Finally, this chapter illustrates the difficulty of improving highway safety with a seat belt law with weak enforcement provisions. Another factor is the composition of the groups not using the seat belt: very young drivers and males.[46] These groups have a much higher probability of being involved in an accident than females and older drivers. As in other localities, these lower risk drivers are more likely to use the seat belt. As in California, more efforts must be made to reach high-risk groups in order to lower fatalities further. Also, the smaller number of fatalities as opposed to a larger number of injuries probably masks some beneficial impact of the Michigan seat belt law.[47]

Perhaps the seat belt law does not greatly decrease highway casualties when other effective interventions precede the law. However, the laws in Great Britain and New York, with their primary enforcement, clearly are more successful than those in Michigan and California, even though both New York and Great Britain also instituted other safety improvements in addition to their seat belt laws.

# 8

## *IMPLICATIONS FOR PUBLIC POLICY*

*THERE ARE* important differences between Great Britain's drinking-driving reform and that in the United States. Drinking-driving laws in England and Wales fit the classic definition of deterrence, as discussed in chapter 2. The 1983 Christmas Crusade was followed by a temporary lessening in fatalities and serious injuries, which dissipated after a few months.

On the other hand, the public in England and Wales had few problems adjusting to the 1983 seat belt law. A high compliance rate greatly reduced casualties. The U.S. states presented nearly the opposite result, in contrast to expectation. A more permanent casualty decline was found in the states following the passage of drinking and driving reform, while consistent results for the seat belt law was more problematic. Only in New York State, with primary enforcement, did fatalities drop significantly.

As with seat belt use, culture may be a major explanatory variable with regard to drinking and driving when one compares the United States and Britain. For example, broad concern with alcohol abuse, underage drinking, and health in general seems much stronger in the United States than in Great Britain. Britain may have been in the forefront of nations in the battle against drinking and driving during the 1960s, but in recent years it has probably lagged behind the United States on this issue. While the United States has recently restricted alcohol by raising the drinking age, taxing alcohol more heavily, and restricting happy hours, in Great Britain the pubs have extended their hours and continue to be used as centers for social drinking most evenings. The drinking age is maintained at eighteen. Also, there is probably less emphasis on health in general in Britain. Smoking continues to be widely tolerated in public areas, and exercise clubs and physical fitness facilities are much less apparent in London than in Washington, D.C., or Los Angeles.

## *DRINKING-DRIVING REFORM*

The current American preoccupation with health, drinking and driving, and alcohol and drug abuse makes the new drinking-driving laws difficult to interpret with conventional time-series analysis.[1] On the other hand, these laws have lowered fatalities considerably and over a longer period than was evident in earlier studies. The success of these laws lies largely in the new awareness in the United States of the disastrous effects of mixing alcohol with driving. In fact, some analysts claim that it is difficult to detect whether the laws influence drinking and driving or whether drinking and driving produces the laws.[2] "So much is happening to improve automobile safety and to diminish consumption of alcohol, especially among the young, that it is too early to have any conclusion about the relative role of increased severity of punishment in affecting a decrease in automobile fatalities."[3]

On this point I take issue. Although it is reasonable to view the new drinking-driving laws as products of increased public awareness, I demonstrate here that the laws in themselves effect change at the time of their passage. This is especially true in New York and California, where abrupt shifts in the series occurred at the time of implementation. Also, when influences such as number of miles driven, economic conditions, mandatory seat belt use, and changes in the minimum legal drinking age were controlled, drinking-driving reforms had a consistent effect on fatalities. However, the new awareness is probably responsible for maintaining the benefits of the laws.

More specifically, with regard to policy formulation, this book demonstrates that laws governing the alcohol-impaired driver are more likely to work if they move beyond the concept of simple deterrence. While an increase in punishment is an important component of these cases, it is certainty of punishment that makes them particularly effective. For example, Michigan did not raise penalties in terms of fines, but it raised the possibility of license suspension, even for drivers with blood-alcohol concentrations under 0.10. Many prosecutors in the state traded severity for celerity—a lesser charge was accepted in exchange for a guilty plea. Not only did this avoid the unpleasant side effect of slowing the judicial process, as in California, but also fatalities remained low despite plea bargaining. The Michigan experience parallels that of Finland, where road fatalities declined even though severity of punishment was reduced by a 1977 law.[4] The key element in both cases is certainty of punishment.

The practical lesson for policy makers is that reductions in highway fatalities will not result from legislation that concentrates only on severity of punishment. States that raise penalties for alcohol-impaired driving and experience few favorable consequences may wish to focus on certainty and celerity of punishment in any new legislation. For example, in Georgia, fines for driving under the influence were increased under a 1983 law, but first offenders are usually able to plea bargain and to retain an unrestricted driver's license. Perhaps a more effective penalty than higher fines is a short period of driver's license suspension. Citizen activists may wish to focus on such provisions. However, laws that penalize by license suspension must be consistent and applied uniformly.[5] In addition, many drivers whose license is suspended or revoked will drive anyway, with a low probability of punishment. For many drivers, the cost of not driving is much higher than the small risk of apprehension.

Despite increased awareness of the problems of drinking and driving in the United States in the early 1980s, some survey research documents that Americans are well behind Europeans in their knowledge about the specifics of drinking-driving legislation. Norwegians, for example, are much more knowledgeable than Americans about the concept of blood-alcohol concentration, per se laws, and the possible penalties for violation.[6] Whilc 72 percent of Norwegians know the consequences for a first offender, only 14 percent of Americans do. Americans are thus unlikely to respond to specific provisions of drinking-driving legislation. Lowering the blood-alcohol concentration necessary for a conviction probably will not reduce the casualties brought on by drunken driving. In fact, such legislation may simply alienate social drinkers by criminalizing their behavior.[7]

Perhaps ignorance of the law helps to explain the deterrent effect of California's drinking-driving law. While the possibility of a jail sentence is an important part of the legislative package, this option is not used routinely for first offenders. Still, the law exhibits a significant beneficial effect, and it may be that drivers are deterred by the perception that punishment might include jail sentences. While certainty of punishment is more likely in California, crowded courts make celerity of punishment less likely. The California case illustrates that even the perception of severity of punishment involves a trade-off with swiftness of punishment—a goal that groups such as Mothers Against Drunk Driving (MADD) hold important.

Of the U.S. states considered in this book, New York best exemplifies the traditional theory of deterrence—the notion that increased punishment results in a lower level of drinking and driving. Yet the New York analysis illustrates that vigorous enforcement, widespread publicity, and political leadership also are necessary to make tougher laws succeed. Without the broad visibility and support that drinking-driving statutes gained in the state, it is unlikely that many drivers know the penalties for violation. In addition, local governments are given strong financial incentives to cooperate in the program, greatly stimulating enforcement. At the very least, the publicity in New York makes it improbable that drivers do not know that penalties for drunk driving are more severe than formerly. Even in this state, certainty that the laws will be enforced and that drivers will be punished is probably a better explanation for the safety benefits realized than severity of punishment.

### *Changes in Driving Practices*

It appears that 1986 was a watershed year for the United States in traffic safety policy. By the year's end, most states had passed drinking-driving legislation, most had raised the legal drinking age to twenty-one, and most had passed seat belt laws. But rumblings of discontent were evident by this point. In the 1986 election, both Nebraska and Massachusetts repealed their seat belt laws in statewide referenda. Also, fatality rates began to rise across the nation. Several states, including California, permitted a sixty-five-mile-per-hour speed limit on rural interstate highways.

It may take more time to comprehend the effects of the new speed limits fully, but it is difficult to imagine that they have a favorable effect on safety.[8] Moreover, a spillover effect should be apparent to anyone driving on interstate highways outside of rural areas. When driving fifty-five miles per hour on interstate highways in urban areas such as Atlanta, Chicago, or Los Angeles, one is likely to be run off the road by drivers traveling at higher speeds. High-speed driving on the interstates also may accelerate the speed on roads less suited for rapidly moving traffic, increasing safety risks significantly. In addition, the most high-risk drivers are the ones who increase their speeds: the young, those with prior citations, and those riding alone.[9] So while the public has been sensitized to the drinking-driving problem and has made appropriate adjustments in many localities, the public is not convinced of the dangers of speed and is largely unwilling to make even elementary adjustments to the new limits by wearing seat belts.

The new discontent on the part of citizens is understandable; traditionally, Americans do not like government regulation in any aspect of their lives. But if the problem of traffic fatalities is viewed as a combination of many factors in addition to drinking and driving, there is a need for legislation to be consistent and to be prosafety. If it is not, reforms in one area, such as drinking and driving or the legal drinking age, are likely to be offset by weakly enforced seat belt laws and higher speed limits.

### *The Minimum Legal Drinking Age*

Reforms in drinking ages already have been accomplished in the United States. The limited instances examined show that these reforms had a greater impact on fatalities when the age was raised comprehensively, as in Michigan, than incrementally, as in New York. Fatality reduction appears stronger when the age change comes first in the policy cycle. It is particularly difficult to effect fatalities with drinking-age reform if another reform (such as drinking-driving legislation) lowers fatalities initially. The research reveals more about the consequences of changing the drinking age than about an ideal drinking age. It is highly unlikely that the legal drinking age will be changed in the near future, but if any lowering of the legal age is attempted, it should be done gradually.

More important in terms of advice to policy makers, a high legal drinking age in and of itself is not sufficient to address the problem of highway fatalities among young drivers. In terms of measurable impact, the drinking-driving reforms in both Michigan and California affect the young favorably. Results are especially impressive in California, where the drinking age of twenty-one is the rule. To improve on the number of fatalities among the youngest drivers, attempts also must be made to develop driving skills, educate young people about the dangers of alcohol, and provide more alcohol-free recreational opportunities in the evening hours. The latter option may provide alternatives to cruising on highways or in shopping centers—environments that encourage illegal, underage drinking. Some thought might also be given to providing curfews for younger drivers, particularly on weekends. Indeed, one of the reasons for the seeming ineffectiveness of the New York drinking-age interventions may be the fewer number of young drivers on the road at night due to curfew hours.

Similarly, states might experiment with licensing drivers at a slightly later age, as in New York. Fewer youngsters will drive illegally than will drink illegally. More consideration also should be given to allowing some alcohol consumption prior to age twenty-one, such as parentally supervised drinking in the home or in restaurants. While I find no adverse effects for twenty-one-year-olds throughout this study when the drinking age is changed, a minimum of underage drinking should be tolerated to avoid the shock effect of attaining the legal age. Because of liability issues and potential abuses, adult-supervised drinking could be limited to parents or guardians in the home and to restaurants as an accompaniment to meals. Many may find these alternatives distasteful, but one must balance them against the inability of many young people to handle alcohol and the ineffectiveness of prohibitions.

### *Seat Belt Laws*

The seat belt and its underutilization is one area of missed policy potential.[10] Even New York State, whose mandatory use law has a beneficial effect on fatalities, has a long-term compliance rate of less than 50 percent. Seat belt use in the United States, compared to Europe, is a cultural problem and is difficult to explain directly.[11] Perhaps American individualism and the decentralized structure of law enforcement make it difficult for citizens to accept a highly beneficial device, such as the seat belt, even in states with primary enforcement. The resistance to the laws make future options difficult for policy makers. While a majority of states have passed mandatory use laws, their provisions are weak and fail to meet U.S. Department of Transportation recommendations. For this reason, air bags have been installed in American cars beginning with 1990 models.

The passage of primary enforcement laws is important, yet the impact of the laws themselves on fatalities is indirect. Whether enforcement is primary or secondary, motorists must comply for the laws to be effective. If compliance is high, casualties will be reduced. Beyond the passage of new primary-enforcement legislation and the amendment of existing secondary-enforcement laws, other measures policy makers can use to encourage wearing the seat belt are education for high-risk groups, penalties on the driver's license, and the amendment of insurance policies to encourage belt wearing.[12]

## *CONCLUSION*

In spite of the necessity of additional reforms and the growing public sentiment against government regulation in highway safety, considerable improvements are evident in the United States. Most important is the attitude that may best be described as general prevention.[13] While the American public has not completely accepted this notion with regard to the seat belt, attitudes have been transformed with regard to the drinking driver. Clearly, alcohol-impaired driving, once accepted as a part of everyday life, is regarded adversely as a social norm. An environment has been created that holds that safety and physical well-being are more significant than the social gains of drinking and driving.

Automobile and highway safety will be enhanced further by advances in technology such as performance and breath test interlocks and improvements in the devices to detect and apprehend drinking drivers.[14] However, the most important factor in safe driving is an attitude about prevention that comprehends the human potential to avoid casualties in the long term. While this book may show cause for some optimism, it remains to be seen if this attitude can be maintained into the 1990s.

*Appendix*
*Notes*
*Index*

# APPENDIX

TABLE A-1
IMPACT OF THE 1983 SEAT BELT LAW ON FATAL OR SERIOUS CASUALTIES IN ENGLAND AND WALES

| | *Car Casualties (treatment)* | | *Noncar Casualties (control)* | |
|---|---|---|---|---|
| | *Estimate* | *t-score* | *Estimate* | *t-score* |
| Constant | 2,514.03 | 25.70 | 3,914.79 | 24.85 |
| AR (1) | 0.294 | 3.16 | 0.515 | 6.32 |
| AR (1) (12) | 0.757 | 10.68 | 0.738 | 10.67 |
| Seat belt law | −453.51 | −5.51 | −371.55 | −2.53 |
| Christmas Crusade | −438.64 | −2.74 | 138.94 | 0.69 |
| Number of unemployed | 0.019 | 0.48 | −0.013 | −0.25 |

TABLE A-2
IMPACT OF THE 1983 SEAT BELT LAW ON NONSERIOUS CASUALTIES IN ENGLAND AND WALES

| | *Car Casualties (treatment)* | | *Noncar Casualties (control)* | |
|---|---|---|---|---|
| | *Estimate* | *t-score* | *Estimate* | *t-score* |
| Constant | 9,080.21 | 20.42 | 10,583.60 | 25.63 |
| AR (1) | 0.400 | 4.30 | 0.578 | 7.48 |
| AR (1) (12) | 0.704 | 8.58 | 0.777 | 11.84 |
| Seat belt law | −397.91 | −1.02 | −721.71 | −1.86 |
| Christmas Crusade | −1,194.89 | −1.75 | 431.91 | 0.92 |
| Number of unemployed | 0.053 | 0.31 | −0.076 | −0.58 |

TABLE A-3
IMPACT OF THE 1983 SEAT BELT LAW ON FATAL AND SERIOUS SINGLE-VEHICLE ACCIDENTS ON WEEKEND NIGHTS IN ENGLAND AND WALES

| | *Estimate* | *t-score* |
|---|---|---|
| AR (1) | −0.662 | −6.59 |
| AR (2) | −0.418 | −4.15 |
| AR (1) (12) | 0.508 | 4.86 |
| Seat belt law | −103.87 | −3.45 |
| Christmas Crusade | −22.82 | −0.69 |
| Number of unemployed | 0.018 | −1.41 |

TABLE A-4
IMPACT OF NEW YORK STATE POLICY INTERVENTIONS ON TRAFFIC FATALITIES

| | *Estimate* | *t-score* |
|---|---|---|
| AR (1) (12) | −0.505 | −6.20 |
| DWI reform | −28.16 | −4.11 |
| MLDA 18 to 19 | −7.51 | −1.19 |
| Seat belt law | −5.80 | −0.93 |
| MLDA 19 to 21 | 16.44 | 2.38 |
| Miles driven | 4.142E-06 | 1.01 |
| Unemployment rate | −0.682 | −0.31 |

TABLE A-5

IMPACT OF NEW YORK STATE POLICY INTERVENTIONS ON TRAFFIC FATALITIES, SINGLE AND MULTIPLE VEHICLES, DAYTIME AND NIGHTTIME

| | *Male Drivers, Nighttime Single-Vehicle Fatalities* | | *All Drivers, Daytime* | | | |
|---|---|---|---|---|---|---|
| | | | *Single-Vehicle Fatalities* | | *Single- and Multiple-Vehicle Fatalities* | |
| | *Estimate* | *t-score* | *Estimate* | *t-score* | *Estimate* | *t-score* |
| Constant | | | | | 67.09 | 3.50 |
| AR (1) (12) | −0.596 | −6.69 | −0.403 | −4.61 | 0.500 | 6.38 |
| AR (2) (24) | −0.407 | −4.35 | | | | |
| DWI reform | −0.311 | −2.88 | −6.00 | −2.24 | −10.45 | −2.77 |
| MLDA 18 to 19 | −0.023 | −0.23 | 3.44 | 1.37 | 3.40 | 0.87 |
| Seat belt law | −0.209 | −2.01 | −2.01 | −0.80 | −1.16 | −0.24 |
| MLD 19 to 21 | 0.170 | 1.50 | 4.81 | 1.76 | 3.44 | 0.79 |
| Miles driven | 1.484E-08 | 0.24 | 2.380E-06 | 1.44 | 1.507E-08 | 0.79 |
| Unemployed rate | −0.008 | −0.22 | 1.45 | 1.67 | −1.10 | −0.85 |

NOTE: Single-vehicle fatalities for males at nighttime is estimated in logarithmic form.

TABLE A-6
IMPACT OF NEW YORK STATE POLICY INTERVENTIONS ON TRAFFIC FATALITIES, FRONT AND BACK SEAT PASSENGER

| | *Front Seat (including drivers)* | | *Back Seat* | |
|---|---|---|---|---|
| | *Estimate* | *t-score* | *Estimate* | *t-score* |
| Constant | | | 3.70 | 12.97 |
| AR (1) | | | 0.160 | 1.91 |
| AR (1) (12) | −0.411 | −4.88 | 0.398 | 4.78 |
| DWI reform | −0.194 | −3.19 | −0.174 | −2.80 |
| MLDA 18 to 19 | −0.049 | −0.87 | −0.047 | −0.70 |
| Seat belt law | −0.102 | −1.83 | −0.013 | −0.20 |
| MLDA 19 to 21 | 0.092 | 1.48 | 0.080 | 1.11 |
| Miles driven | 5.623E-08 | 1.52 | 6.773E-08 | 2.48 |
| Unemployment rate | −0.017 | −0.86 | 0.017 | 0.85 |

NOTE: Fatalities are estimated in logarithmic form.

TABLE A-7
IMPACT OF CALIFORNIA POLICY INTERVENTIONS ON TRAFFIC FATALITIES

| | *Estimate* | *t-score* |
|---|---|---|
| MA (1) | 0.862 | 17.04 |
| MA (1) (12) | 0.773 | 13.46 |
| DUI reform | −28.49 | −2.00 |
| Seat belt law | 4.17 | 0.30 |
| Miles driven | 3.0000038 | 1.32 |
| Unemployment rate | −2.54 | −0.98 |

TABLE A-8

IMPACT OF CALIFORNIA POLICY INTERVENTIONS ON TRAFFIC FATALITIES, SINGLE AND MULTIPLE VEHICLES, DAYTIME AND NIGHTTIME

| | *Male Drivers, Nighttime Single-Vehicle Fatalities* | | *All Drivers, Daytime* | | | |
|---|---|---|---|---|---|---|
| | | | *Single-Vehicle Fatalities* | | *Single- and Multiple-Vehicle Fatalities* | |
| | *Estimate* | *t-score* | *Estimate* | *t-score* | *Estimate* | *t-score* |
| Constant | 3.37 | 11.62 | | | | |
| MA (1) | | | | | 0.909 | 22.08 |
| MA (1) (12) | −0.144 | −1.72 | 0.832 | 16.43 | 0.854 | 16.29 |
| DUI reform | −0.238 | −3.47 | 1.81 | 0.40 | −11.65 | −1.41 |
| Seat belt law | −0.114 | −1.86 | −0.097 | −0.03 | 3.89 | 0.52 |
| Miles driven | 4.121E-08 | 2.68 | −3.16 | −3.42 | 1.861E-06 | 1.04 |
| Unemployed rate | −0.004 | −0.31 | −7.231E-08 | −0.07 | 0.0097 | 0.01 |

NOTE: Single-vehicle fatalities for males at nighttime is estimated in logarithmic form.

TABLE A-9
IMPACT OF CALIFORNIA POLICY INTERVENTIONS ON TRAFFIC FATALITIES, FRONT AND BACK SEAT PASSENGERS

| | *Front Seat (including drivers)* | | *Back Seat* | |
|---|---|---|---|---|
| | *Estimate* | *t-score* | *Estimate* | *t-score* |
| MA (1) | 0.838 | 17.62 | | |
| MA (1) (12) | −0.202 | −2.38 | 0.886 | 19.31 |
| DUI reform | −13.21 | −1.16 | −13.76 | −2.90 |
| Seat belt law | −5.46 | −0.52 | 2.89 | 0.86 |
| Miles driven | 7.111E-06 | 4.47 | 1.819E-06 | 1.61 |
| Unemployment rate | −4.32 | −1.91 | 1.13 | −1.18 |

TABLE A-10
IMPACT OF CALIFORNIA POLICY INTERVENTIONS ON TRAFFIC FATALITIES, DRIVER UNDER AGE TWENTY-ONE

| | *All Fatalities* | | *Single-Vehicle Fatalities, Nighttime* | |
|---|---|---|---|---|
| | *Estimate* | *t-score* | *Estimate* | *t-score* |
| Constant | 127.64 | 6.64 | | |
| MA (1) | | | −0.254 | −3.14 |
| MA (2) | | | −0.209 | −2.59 |
| MA (1) (12) | | | −0.241 | −2.86 |
| DUI reform | −17.09 | −3.76 | −7.40 | −2.79 |
| Seat belt law | −4.73 | −1.16 | −2.90 | −0.79 |
| Miles driven | 2.800E-06 | 2.76 | 2.682E-06 | 8.53 |
| Unemployment rate | −4.39 | −4.11 | 0.488 | 0.98 |

TABLE A-11
IMPACT OF MICHIGAN POLICY INTERVENTIONS ON TRAFFIC FATALITIES

| | *Estimate* | *t-score* |
|---|---|---|
| MA (1) (12) | 0.656 | 9.53 |
| AR (1) | 0.239 | 2.81 |
| MLDA 18 to 21 | −11.82 | −3.31 |
| Drinking-driving reform | −14.74 | −2.84 |
| Seat belt law | 1.50 | 0.34 |
| Miles driven | 4.726E-07 | 0.13 |
| Unemployment rate | −2.48 | −4.67 |

TABLE A-12

IMPACT OF POLICY INTERVENTIONS ON MICHIGAN TRAFFIC FATALITIES, SINGLE AND MULTIPLE VEHICLES, DAYTIME AND NIGHTTIME

| | *Male Drivers, Nighttime Single-Vehicle Fatalities* | | *All Drivers, Daytime* | | | |
|---|---|---|---|---|---|---|
| | | | *Single-Vehicle Fatalities* | | *Single- and Multiple-Vehicle Fatalities* | |
| | *Estimate* | *t-score* | *Estimate* | *t-score* | *Estimate* | *t-score* |
| MA (1) (12) | 0.685 | 10.43 | 0.735 | 11.86 | 0.699 | 10.77 |
| MLDA 18 to 21 | −4.16 | −3.10 | −3.62 | −3.14 | −5.82 | −3.12 |
| Drinking-Driving reform | −3.97 | −2.76 | −2.75 | −2.11 | −3.15 | −1.56 |
| Seat belt law | 1.58 | 0.95 | −0.52 | −0.34 | 0.454 | 0.19 |
| Miles driven | −8.143-07 | −0.61 | 1.016E-06 | 0.84 | 2.407E-06 | 1.29 |
| Unemployment rate | 0.2216 | 1.10 | −0.128 | −0.70 | −1.07 | −3.76 |

TABLE A-13
IMPACT OF MICHIGAN POLICY INTERVENTIONS ON TRAFFIC FATALITIES FRONT AND BACK SEAT PASSENGERS

| | *Front Seat (including drivers)* | | *Back Seat* | |
|---|---|---|---|---|
| | *Estimate* | *t-score* | *Estimate* | *t-score* |
| MA (1) (12) | 0.677 | 10.17 | 0.644 | 9.30 |
| MLDA 18 to 21 | −7.17 | −2.68 | −4.55 | −2.48 |
| Drinking-driving reform | −11.00 | −3.80 | −3.71 | −1.87 |
| Seat belt law | 1.97 | 0.59 | −0.388 | −0.17 |
| Miles driven | 2.060E-06 | 3.77 | −1.602E-06 | −0.91 |
| Unemployment rate | −1.77 | −4.37 | −0.706 | −2.62 |

TABLE A-14

IMPACT OF MICHIGAN POLICY INTERVENTIONS ON TRAFFIC FATALITIES, WITH A YOUNG DRIVER

| | *Driver Under Age 21* | | | | *Driver Age 21* | |
|---|---|---|---|---|---|---|
| | *All Fatalities* | | *Single-Vehicle Fatalities* | | *All Fatalities* | |
| | *Estimate* | *t-score* | *Estimate* | *t-score* | *Estimate* | *t-score* |
| MA (1) (12) | 0.640 | 9.17 | 0.655 | 9.32 | 0.662 | 10.07 |
| MLDA 18 to 21 | −9.04 | −4.07 | −5.79 | −3.41 | 0.620 | 0.96 |
| Drinking-driving reform | −7.16 | −3.03 | −4.26 | −2.37 | −0.860 | −1.25 |
| Seat belt law | 1.08 | 0.02 | 2.30 | 1.13 | −0.982 | −1.24 |
| Miles driven | −2.393E-06 | −1.13 | −2.693E-06 | −1.65 | 2.671E-07 | 0.43 |
| Unemployment rate | −1.30 | −3.99 | −0.440 | −1.77 | −0.146 | −1.53 |

# NOTES

## CHAPTER 1. Introduction

1. H. Laurence Ross, "Law, Science and Accidents: The British Road Safety Act of 1967," *Journal of Legal Studies* 2 (1973): 1–78.

2. H. Laurence Ross, *Deterring the Drinking Driver*, revised and updated edition (Lexington, Mass.: Lexington, 1984).

3. H. Laurence Ross and James P. Foley, "Judicial Disobedience of the Mandate to Imprison Drunk Drivers," *Law and Society Review* 21 (1982): 315–23.

4. Ross, *Deterring the Drinking Driver*, 99–100. James B. Jacobs, *Drunk Driving: An American Dilemma* (Chicago: University of Chicago Press, 1989).

5. Peter H. Rossi, James D. Wright, and Sonia R. Wright, "The Theory and Practice of Applied Social Research," *Evaluation Quarterly* 2 (1978): 171–91; Illene N. Bernstein and Howard E. Freeman, *Academic and Entrepreneural Research* (New York: Russell Sage, 1975).

6. Brian A. Jonah and John J. Lawson, "The Effectiveness of the Canadian Mandatory Seat Belt Use Laws," *Accident Analysis and Prevention* 16 (1984): 433–50; Paul M. Hurst, "Compulsory Seatbelt Use: Further Inferences," *Accident Analysis and Prevention* 11 (1979): 27–33; Jerome S. Legge, Jr., "Reforming Public Safety: An Evaluation of the 1983 British Seat Belt Law," *Law and Policy* 9 (1987): 17–36.

7. H. Laurence Ross, "Britain's Christmas Crusade Against Drinking and Driving," *Journal of Studies on Alcohol* 48 (1987): 476–82.

8. Ibid.; Legge, "Reforming Public Safety."

9. A recent and comprehensive treatment of the subject is Alexander C. Wagenaar, Richard G. Maybee, and Kathleen P. Sullivan,

"Mandatory Seat Belt Laws in Eight States: A Time Series Evaluation," *Journal of Safety Research* 19 (1988): 51–70. See also Alexander C. Wagenaar and Richard G. Maybee, "The Legal Minimum Drinking Age in Texas: Effects of an Increase from 18 to 19," *Journal of Safety Research* 17 (1986): 165–78; Peter Asch and David T. Levy, "Does the Minimum Drinking Age Affect Traffic Fatalities?" *Journal of Policy Analysis and Management* 6 (1987): 180–92; Mike A. Males, "The Minimum Purchase Age for Alcohol and Young-Driver Fatal Crashes: A Long-Term View," *Journal of Legal Studies* 25 (1986): 181–211; Philip J. Cook and George Tauchen, "The Effects of Minimum Drinking Age Legislation on Youthful Auto Fatalities, 1970–1977," *Journal of Legal Studies* 23 (1984): 169–90; Allan F. Williams, Paul L. Zador, Sandra S. Harris, and Ronald S. Karpf, "The Effect of Raising the Legal Minimum Drinking Age on Involvement in Fatal Crashes," *Journal of Legal Studies* 12 (1983): 169–79; Joel W. Grube and Kathleen A. Kearney, "A 'Mandatory' Jail Sentence for Drinking and Driving," *Evaluation Review* 7 (1983): 235–46; and Ross and Foley, "Judicial Disobedience."

10. Especially important work on Michigan has been undertaken by Alexander C. Wagenaar, *Alcohol, Young Drivers and Traffic Accidents* (Lexington, Mass.: Lexington, 1983); and "Preventing Highway Crashes by Raising the Legal Minimum Age for Drinking: The Michigan Experience 6 Years Later," *Journal of Safety Research* 17 (1986): 101–09.

11. H. Laurence Ross, "Deterring Drunken Driving: An Analysis of Current Efforts," *Journal of Studies on Alcohol,* Supplement 10 (1985): 122–28.

12. For a thorough analysis of the Maine law, see R. Hingson, T. Heeren, D. Kovenock, et al., "Effects of Maine's 1981 and Massachusetts' 1982 Driving-Under-the-Influence Legislation," *American Journal of Public Health* 22 (1987): 593–97.

13. Ibid.; and H. Laurence Ross, "Administrative License Revocation in New Mexico: An Evaluation," *Law and Policy* 9 (1987): 5–16.

14. Franklin E. Zimring, "Law, Society and the Drinking Driver: Some Concluding Reflections," in *Social Control of the Drinking Driver,* ed. Michael D. Laurence, John R. Snortum, and Franklin E. Zimring (Chicago: University of Chicago Press, 1988), 377.

15. Ross, "Law, Science and Accidents."

16. Franklin Zimring and Gordon Hawkins, "The Legal Threat as an Instrument of Social Change," *Journal of Social Issues* 39 (1983): 143–57.

17. Increasingly, the prevention of alcohol-impaired driving and its consequences is viewed as being beyond simple behavioral change of the individual. See Frank A. Haight, "Road Safety: A Perspective and A New Strategy," *Journal of Safety Research* 16 (1985): 91–98; James F. Mosher, "Alcohol Policy and the Presidential Commission on Drunk Driving: The Paths Not Taken," *Accident Analysis and Prevention* 17 (1985): 239–50; and Graeme A. Thomson, "Drinking-Driving Accident Countermeasures: Why Not Try Changing the Environment?" *Accident Analysis and Prevention* 17 (1985): 207–10.

18. H. Laurence Ross and Richard McCleary, "Methods for Studying the Impact of Drunk Driving Laws," *Accident Analysis and Prevention* 15 (1983): 415–28.

19. Central Statistical Office, *Annual Abstract of Statistics* (1986), (London: Her Majesty's Stationery Office, 1985), 198.

## *CHAPTER 2. Deterrence Theory and General Prevention*

1. Jerome S. Legge, Jr., "Reforming Public Safety: An Evaluation of the 1983 British Seat Belt Law," *Law and Policy* 9 (1987): 19–36; and Roy E. L. Watson, "The Effectiveness of Police Enforcement as a General Deterrent," *Law and Society Review* 20 (1986): 293–99.

2. *Social Control of the Drinking Driver,* ed., Michael D. Laurence, John R. Snortum, and Franklin E. Zimring (Chicago: University of Chicago Press, 1988).

3. William S. Chambliss, "The Deterrent Influence of Punishment," *Crime and Delinquency* 12 (1966): 75.

4. Barry Glassner, Margaret Ksander, Bruce Berg, and Bruce D. Johnson, "A Note on the Deterrent Effect of Juvenile vs. Adult Jurisdiction," *Social Problems* 31 (1983): 219–21.

5. Maynard L. Erickson, Mark C. Stafford, and James M. Galliher, "The Normative Erosion Hypothesis: The Latent Consequences of Juvenile Justice Practices," *Sociological Quarterly* 25 (1984): 373–84.

6. H. Francis Pestello, "Deterrence: A Reconceptualization," *Crime and Delinquency* 30 (1984): 593–609.

7. H. Laurence Ross, *Deterring the Drinking Driver,* revised and updated edition (Lexington, Mass.: Lexington, 1984).

8. George S. Bridges and James A. Stone, "Effects of Criminal Punishment on Perceived Threat of Punishment: Toward an Understanding of Specific Deterrence," *Journal of Research in Crime and Delinquency* 23 (1986): 207–39.

9. Ibid., 230.

10. Irving Piliavin, Rosemary Gartner, Craig Thorton, and Ross L. Matgueda, "Crime, Deterrence and Rational Choice," *American Sociological Review* 51 (1986): 101–19.

11. Lawrence W. Sherman and Richard A. Berk, "The Specific Deterrent Effects of Arrest for Domestic Assault," *American Sociological Review* 49 (1984): 262–71.

12. Richard A. Berk and Phyllis J. Newton, "Does Arrest Really Deter Wife Battery? An Effort to Replicate the Findings of the Minneapolis Spouse Abuse Experiment," *American Sociological Review* 50 (1985): 253–62.

13. Scott H. Decker and Carol W. Kohfeld, "Crimes, Crime Rates, Arrests and Arrest Ratios: Implications for Deterrence Theory," *Criminology* 23 (1985): 437–50.

14. Stuart J. Deutsch and Francis B. Alt, "The Effect of Massachusetts' Gun Control Law on Gun-Related Crimes in the City of Boston," *Evaluation Quarterly* 1 (1977): 543–68.

15. Leslie J. McCain and Richard McCleary, "The Statistical Analysis of the Simple Interrupted Time-Series-Quasi-Experiment," in Thomas D. Cook and Donald T. Campbell, eds., *Quasi-Experimentation* (Boston: Houghton-Mifflin, 1979), 233–93.

16. Colin Loftin and David McDowall, "The Deterrent Effects of the Florida Felony Firearm Law," *Journal of Criminal Law and Criminology* 75 (1984): 250–59; quotation at 258.

17. Colin Loftin, Milton Heumann, and David McDowall, "Mandatory Sentencing and Firearms in Detroit: Evaluating an Alternative to Gun Control," *Law and Society Review* 17 (1983): 287–318.

18. Isaac Ehrlich, "The Deterrent Effect of Capital Punishment: A Question of Life and Death," *American Economic Review* 65 (1975): 397–417.

19. Stephen K. Layson, "Another View of the Canadian Time-Series Evidence," *Canadian Journal of Economics* 16 (1983): 52–73;

Kenneth Wolpin, "Capital Punishment and Homicide in England: A Summary of Results," *American Economic Review; Papers and Proceedings* (1978): 422–27.

20. Layson, 70.

21. William C. Bailey, "Disaggregation and Death Penalty Research: The Case of Murder in Chicago," *Journal of Criminal Law and Criminology* 74 (1983): 827–59. Bailey cites a number of works in this area, most of which contradict the findings of Ehrlich. A few of these are William J. Bowers and Glenn L. Pierce, "The Illusion of Deterrence in Isaac Ehrlich's Research on Capital Punishment," *Yale Law Journal* 85 (1975): 187–208; Stephen S. Brier and Stephen E. Feinberg, "Recent Econometric Modeling of Crime and Punishment: Support for the Deterrence Hypothesis?" *Evaluation Review* 4 (1980): 147–91; Brian E. Forst, "The Deterrent Effect of Capital Punishment: A Cross-State Analysis of the 1960s," *Minnesota Law Review* 61 (1977): 743–67; and Peter Passell and John B. Taylor, "The Deterrent Effect of Capital Punishment: Another View," *American Economic Review* 67 (1977): 445–51.

22. Bailey, "Disaggregation and Death Penalty Research."

23. Ibid., 859.

24. William C. Bailey, "Murder and the Death Penalty," *Journal of Criminal Law and Criminology* 65 (1974): 416–23.

25. Dane Archer, Rosemary Gartner, and Marc Beittel, "Homicide and the Death Penalty: A Cross-National Test of a Deterrence Hypothesis," *Journal of Criminal Law and Criminology* 74 (1983): 991–1013.

26. Sam G. McFarland, "Is Capital Punishment a Short-Term Deterrent to Homicide? A Study of the Effects of Four Recent American Executions," *Journal of Criminal Law and Criminology* 74 (1983): 991–1013.

27. The most authoritative source on the drinking and driving question is Ross, *Deterring the Drinking Driver.* A more recent work is Ross Homel, *Policing and Punishing the Drinking Driver* (New York: Springer-Verlag, 1988).

28. See Joseph R. Gusfield, *The Culture of Public Problems: Drinking-Driving and the Symbolic Order* (Chicago: University of Chicago Press, 1981).

29. The discussion of drinking and driving in Scandinavia bor-

rows heavily from Ross, *Deterring the Drinking Driver,* chapter 4. On Scandinavia, see H. Laurence Ross, "The Scandinavian Myth: The Effectiveness of Drinking-and-Driving Legislation in Sweden and Norway," *Journal of Legal Studies* 4 (1975): 285–310; and H. Laurence Ross, Hans Klette, and Richard McCleary, "Liberalization and Rationalization of Drunk-Driving Laws in Scandinavia," *Accident Analysis and Prevention* 16 (1984): 471–87.

30. Ross, *Deterring the Drinking Driver,* 66–70.

31. Ibid., 62–63.

32. Ibid., 68–69; Johannes Andenaes, *Punishment and Deterrence* (Ann Arbor: University of Michigan Press, 1974).

33. Ross has revised his view over the past several years in response to the scholarship of others who have made a more optimistic interpretation of the deterrent effects of the Scandinavian laws. In particular, the following work is useful: John R. Snortum, "Alcohol-Impaired Driving in Norway and Sweden: Another Look at 'the Scandinavian Myth,'" *Law and Policy* 6 (1984): 5–37; a comment by Ross and a rejoinder by Snortum can be found on pages 37–41 and pages 42–43 of the same volume; also see John R. Snortum, "Controlling the Alcohol-Impaired Driver in Scandinavia and the United States: Simple Deterrence and Beyond," *Journal of Criminal Justice* 12 (1984): 131–48.

34. The most comprehensive analysis of effects of the law is H. Laurence Ross, "Law, Science and Accidents: The British Road Safety Act of 1967," *Journal of Legal Studies* 2 (1973): 1–78; My description of the provisions of the act relies on this source and also on Ross, *Deterring the Drinking Driver,* 24–34.

35. Ross, *Deterring the Drinking Driver,* 25.

36. Ibid., 34. A more pessimistic assessment of the Road Safety Act was made by Llad Phillips, Subhash Ray, and Harold L. Votey, Jr., "Forecasting Highway Safety: The British Road Safety Act and a Sense of Déjà Vu," *Journal of Criminal Justice* 12 (1984): 101–14.

37. Ross, *Deterring the Drinking Driver,* 37. My description of the provisions of the act rely on this source.

38. H. Laurence Ross, Richard McCleary, and Thomas Epperlein, "Deterrence of Drinking and Driving in France: An Evaluation of the Law of July 12, 1978," *Law and Society Review* 16 (1981–82): 345–74.

39. See Ross, *Deterring the Drinking Driver,* 42–60.

40. Ibid., 91–94.

41. Ross, Klette and McCleary, "Liberalization and Rationalization of Drunk-Driving Laws," 471–87. Another good study of severe punishment in the United States is Leon Robertson, Robert F. Rich, and H. Laurence Ross, "Jail Sentences for Driving While Intoxicated in Chicago: A Judicial Policy that Failed," *Law and Society Review* 8 (1973): 55–67.

42. Joel W. Grube and Kathleen A. Kearney, "A 'Mandatory' Jail Sentence for Drinking and Driving," *Evaluation Review* 7 (1983): 235–46.

43. Ross, *Deterring the Drinking Driver,* 118–21.

44. R. Peck, "The Traffic Safety Impact of California's New Drunk Driving Law (AB 541): An Evaluation of the First Nine Months of Experience" (Sacramento: State of California Department of Motor Vehicles, 1983, mimeographed). Although fatalities did not decrease, there was a temporary improvement in nighttime injury crashes. Log-linear analysis and not interrupted time series was the methodology employed.

45. Michael E. Hilton, "The Impact of Recent Changes in California Drinking-Driving Laws on Fatal Accident Levels During the First Postintervention Year: An Interrupted Time Series Analysis," *Law and Society Review* 18 (1984): 605–27.

46. Ross, *Deterring the Drinking Driver,* 119–20.

47. R. K. Jones, H. C. Joksch, J. C. Lacy, and H. J. Schmidt, *Field Evaluation of Jail Sanctions for DWI* (Washington, D.C.: National Highway Traffic Safety Administration, 1988), 69.

48. Carol L. Falkowski, "The Impact of 2-Day Jail Sentences for Drunk Driving in Hennepin County, Minnesota," *Journal of Safety Research* 17 (1986): 33–42.

49. For a comprehensive discussion of the Cheshire experience, see H. Laurence Ross, "Deterrence Regained: The Cheshire Constabulary's 'Breathalyzer Blitz,'" *Journal of Legal Studies* 6 (1977): 403–13.

50. Robert B. Voas and Janet M. Hause, "Deterring the Drinking Driver: The Stockton Experience," *Accident Analysis and Prevention* 19 (1987): 81–90.

51. H. Laurence Ross, "Deterring Drunken Driving: An Analysis of

Current Efforts," *Journal of Studies on Alcohol,* Supplement 10 (1985): 122–28.

52. Ibid., 126.

53. Ross, *Deterring the Drinking Driver,* 121–22.

54. H. Laurence Ross, "Administrative License Revocation in New Mexico: An Evaluation," *Law and Policy* 9 (1987): 5–16.

55. Ibid.

56. I defer discussion of the Michigan law until chapter 7.

57. David F. Preusser, Richard D. Blomberg, and Robert G. Ulmer, "Evaluation of the 1982 Wisconsin Drinking and Driving Law," *Journal of Safety Research* 19 (1988): 29–40.

58. Phillips, Ray, and Votey, "Forecasting Highway Safety"; and Jacqueline Cohen, "The Legal Control of Drunken Driving: A Comment on the Methodological Concerns in Assessing Deterrent Effectiveness," *Journal of Criminal Justice* 12 (1984): 149–54.

59. Snortum, "Controlling the Alcohol-Impaired Driver"; and "Alcohol-Impaired Driving in Norway and Sweden."

60. Snortum, "Controlling the Alcohol-Impaired Driver," 140–48.

61. Ibid.; T. Norström, "Drunken Driving: A Tentative Causal Model," *Scandinavian Studies in Criminology* 6 (1978): 69–78.

62. A good overall description of the problem is D. R. Mayhew, A. C. Donelson, D. J. Beirness, and H. M. Simpson, "Youth, Alcohol and Relative Risk of Crash Involvement," *Accident Analysis and Prevention* 18 (1986): 273–87.

63. While Timothy Williams and Robert Lillis found support for this hypothesis with regard to consumption in New York State, Ralph Hingson et al. found no evidence of reduced fatalities for the youngest groups after the passage of a minimum legal drinking age law in Massachusetts in 1979. See Timothy P. Williams and Robert P. Lillis, "Changes in Alcohol Consumption by 18-Year-Olds Following an Increase in New York State's Purchase Use to 19," *Journal of Studies on Alcohol* 47 (1986): 290–96; Ralph W. Hingson et al., "Impact of Legislation Raising the Legal Drinking Age in Massachusetts from 18 to 20," *American Journal of Public Health* 73 (1983): 163–69.

64. Alexander C. Wagenaar, *Alcohol, Young Drivers and Traffic Accidents* (Lexington, Mass.: Lexington, 1983).

65. R. Douglass and J. Freedman, *Alcohol-Related Casualties and Alcohol Beverage Market Response to Beverage Alcohol Availability Policies*

*in Michigan* (Ann Arbor: University of Michigan Highway Safety Research Institute, 1977). This work is cited in Alexander C. Wagenaar, "Preventing Highway Crashes by Raising the Legal Minimum Age for Drinking: The Michigan Experience 6 Years Later," *Journal of Safety Research* 17 (1986): 102.

66. Wagenaar, "Preventing Highway Crashes," 102.

67. Alexander C. Wagenaar and Richard G. Maybee, "The Legal Minimum Drinking Age in Texas: Effects of an Increase from 18 to 19," *Journal of Safety Research* 17 (1986): 165–78.

68. Allan F. Williams, Paul L. Zador, Sandra S. Harris, and Ronald S. Karpf, "The Effect of Raising the Minimum Legal Drinking Age on Involvement in Fatal Crashes," *Journal of Legal Studies* 12 (1983): 169–79. For other literature that supports the positive effects of a higher minimum age, see Evelyn R. Vingilis and Katherine DeGenova, "Youth and thc Forbidden Fruit: Experiences with Changes in Legal Drinking Age in North America," *Journal of Criminal Justice* 12 (1984): 161–72; P. Hoxie and D. Skinner, *A Statistical Analysis of the Effects of a Uniform Minimum Drinking Age,* National Highway Traffic Safety Administration, Final Report, January 1975–December 1985; (Washington, D.C.: U.S. Department of Transportation); Alan F. Hoskin, Don Yalung-Matthews, and Barbara Carraro, "The Effect of Raising the Legal Minimum Drinking Age on Fatal Crashes in 10 States," *Journal of Safety Research* 17 (1986): 117–21.

69. Mike A. Males, "The Minimum Purchase Age for Alcohol and Young-Driver Fatal Crashes: A Long-Term View," *Journal of Legal Studies* 15 (1986): 181–211.

70. Ibid., 198.

71. Allan F. Williams, "Comment on Males," *Journal of Legal Studies* 15 (1986): 213–17.

72. Peter Asch and David T. Levy, "Does the Minimum Drinking Age Affect Traffic Fatalities?" *Journal of Policy Analysis and Management* 6 (1987): 180–92.

73. Leonard Evans, "Young Driver Involvement in Severe Car Crashes," *Alcohol, Drugs and Driving* 3 (1987): 63–78.

74. The high risk of youths driving at night is documented in Allan F. Williams, "Nighttime Driving and Fatal Crash Involvement of Teenagers," *Accident Analysis and Prevention* 17 (1985): 1–5.

75. The prohibition against late night driving and a higher age for

licensure may help explain the weak effects of the change in the minimum legal drinking age in New York (chapter 5). With regard to driving restriction for youths in New York, see Allan F. Williams, Adrian K. Lund, and David F. Preusser, "Night Driving Curfews in New York and Louisiana: Results of a Questionnaire Survey," *Accident Analysis and Prevention* 17 (1985): 135–45. For articles that deal with this topic more generally, see Ronald S. Karpf and Allan F. Williams, "Teenage Drivers and Motor Vehicle Deaths," *Accident Analysis and Prevention* 15 (1983): 55–63; and Leon S. Robertson, "Patterns of Teenaged Driver Involvement in Fatal Motor Vehicle Crashes: Implications for Policy Change," *Journal of Health Politics, Policy and Law* 6 (1981): 303–14.

76. M. Kirsten Bradstock et al., "Drinking-Driving and Health Lifestyle in the United States: Behavioral Risk Factors Surveys," *Journal of Studies on Alcohol* 48 (1987): 147–51.

77. See Leonard Evans, "The Effectiveness of Seat Belts in Preventing Fatalities," *Accident Analysis and Prevention* 18 (1986): 229–41; Leonard Evans and Michael C. Frick. "Seat Belt Effectiveness in Preventing Driver Fatalities Versus a Number of Vehicular, Accident, Roadway and Environmental Factors," *Journal of Safety Research* 17 (1986): 145–54; and Leonard Evans, "Belted and Unbelted Driver Accident Rates Compared," *Journal of Safety Research* 18 (1987): 57–64.

78. See B. J. Campbell and F. A. Campbell, *Seat Belt Experience in Four Foreign Countries Compared to the United States* (Falls Church, Va.: AAA Foundation for Traffic Safety, 1986). The primary countries analyzed are Australia, Sweden, West Germany, and Great Britain. All of these nations demonstrate much higher compliance than the American States.

79. Legge, "Reforming Public Safety," 18–21.

80. The scenario was developed by Paul Sabatier and Daniel Mazmanian, "The Implementation of Public Policy: A Framework of Analysis," *Policy Studies Journal* 8 (1980): 538–60.

81. Brian A. Jonah and John J. Lawson, "The Effectiveness of the Canadian Mandatory Seat Belt Use Laws," *Accident Analysis and Prevention* 16 (1984): 433–50.

82. Legge, "Reforming Public Safety," 20. Earlier analyses of the British seat belt law that also show reductions in fatalities are

M. Mackay, "Seat Belt Use Under Voluntary and Mandatory Conditions and its Effects on Casualties," in *Symposium on Human Behavior and Traffic Safety* (Warren, Mich.: General Motors Research Laboratories, 1984): 259–83; and G. Pye and E. A. Waters, "Effect of Seat Belt Legislation on Injuries and Road Traffic Accidents in Nottingham," *British Journal of Medicine* 288 (1984): 756–57.

83. Eric A. Latimer and Lester B. Lave, "Initial Effects of the New York State Auto Safety Belt Law," *American Journal of Public Health* 77 (1987): 183–86.

84. Adrian K. Lund, Jessica Pollner, and Allan F. Williams, "Preliminary Estimates of the Effects of Mandatory Seat Belt Use Laws," *Accident Analysis and Prevention* 19 (1987): 219–23.

85. Alexander C. Wagenaar, Richard G. Maybee, and Kathleen P. Sullivan, "Mandatory Seat Belt Laws in Eight States: A Time-Series Evaluation," *Journal of Safety Research* 19 (1988): 51–70.

86. Highway Safety Research Center, *1985–1986 Experience with Belt Laws in the United States* (Chapel Hill: University of North Carolina, 1987).

87. Additional sources that deal with impact on injuries and fatalities in the American States include P. Hoxie and B. Skinner, "Fatality Reductions from Mandatory Seatbelt Usage Laws," in *Restraint Technologies: Front Seat Occupant Protection* (Warrendale, Pa.: Society of Automobile Engineers, 1987), 199–203; Allan F. Williams, Jo Ann K. Wells, and Adrian K. Lund, "Shoulder Belt Use in Four States with Belt Use Laws," *Accident Analysis and Prevention* 19 (1987): 251–60; Alexander C. Wagenaar, Richard G. Maybee, and Kathleen P. Sullivan, *Michigan's Compulsory Restraint Use Policies: Effects on Injuries and Deaths* (Ann Arbor: University of Michigan Transportation Research Institute, 1987): and Adrian K. Lund, Paul Zador, and Jessica Pollner, *Motor Vehicle Occupant Fatalities in Four States with Seat Belt Use Laws* (Washington, D.C.: Insurance Institute for Highway Safety, 1986).

88. Bradstock et al., "Drinking-Driving and Health Lifestyle," 147.

89. David F. Preusser, Adrian K. Lund, Allan F. Williams, and Richard D. Blomberg, "The Effect of New York's Seat Belt Use Law on Teenage Drivers," *Accident Analysis and Prevention* 19 (1987): 73–80.

90. David F. Preusser, Adrian K. Lund, Allan F. Williams, and Richard D. Blomberg, "Belt Use by Higher Risk Drivers Before and

After New York's Seat Belt Law," *Accident Analysis and Prevention* 20 (1988): 245–50; see also Adrian K. Lund, "Voluntary Seat Belt Use Among U.S. Drivers: Geographic, Socioeconomic and Demographic Variation," *Accident Analysis and Prevention* 18 (1986): 43–50.

91. Bradstock et al., "Drinking-Driving and Health Lifestyle," 147.

92. E. Scott Geller et al., "Employer-Based Programs to Motivate Safety Belt Use: A Review of Short-Term and Long-Term Effects," *Journal of Safety Research* 18 (1987): 1–18.

93. William W. Hunter, B. J. Campbell, and J. Richard Stewart, "Seat Belts Pay Off: The Evaluation of a Community-Wide Incentive Program," *Journal of Safety Research* 17 (1986): 23–31.

94. Gary D. Nelson and Patricia B. Moffit, "Seat Belt Promotion: Theory and Practice," *Accident Analysis and Prevention* 20 (1988): 27–36.

95. Watson, "The Effectiveness of Police Enforcement."

96. Jonah and Lawson, "Effectiveness of the Canadian Mandatory Seat Belt Use Law."

97. Information was obtained from "Canada Credits High Belt Use Rates to Publicity, Enforcement"; and "In the Netherlands, a Seat Belt Campaign Is Highly Successful," *Status Report,* June 4, 1988 (Washington, D.C.: Insurance Institute for Highway Safety).

98. Highway Safety Research Center, *1985–1986 Experience with Belt Laws in the United States* (Chapel Hill: University of North Carolina, 1987).

99. Gusfield, *Culture of Public Problems,* 122.

100. Franklin Zimring and Gordon Hawkins, "The Legal Threat as an Instrument of Social Change," *Journal of Social Issues* 39 (1983): 143–57.

101. Ibid., 147.

102. A number of surveys have demonstrated that respondents are knowledgeable about the potential benefits of seat belts but they do not necessarily behave in accordance with their beliefs. For example, see Suzette Morelock, Ralph W. Hingson, Robert A. Smith, and Ruth I. Lederman, "Mandatory Seat Belt Law Support and Opposition in New England—A Survey," *Public Health Reports* 100 (1985): 357–63.

103. Howard Leichter, "Lives, Liberty, and Seat Belts in Britain: Lessons for the United States," *International Journal of Health Services* 16 (1986): 213–26.

104. Ross, *Deterring the Drinking Driver,* 105–06.

105. H. Laurence Ross and James P. Foley, "Judicial Disobedience of the Mandate to Imprison Drunk Drivers," *Law and Society Review* 21 (1982): 315–23.

106. Zimring and Hawkins, "Legal Threat," 148.

107. Paul L. Zador, Adrian K. Lund, Michele Fields, and Karen Weinberg, *Fatal Crash Involvement and Laws Against Alcohol-Impaired Driving* (Washington, D.C.: Insurance Institute for Highway Safety, 1988).

108. For example, see Thomas Epperlein, "Initial Deterrent Effect of the Crackdown on Drinking Drivers in the State of Arizona," *Accident Analysis and Prevention* 19 (1987): 285–303. The Epperlein study, however, does raise the possibility of drivers being deterred due to the publicity surrounding the law.

109. Thomas D. Cook and Donald T. Campbell, *Quasi-Experimentation: Design and Analysis Issues for Field Settings* (Boston: Houghton-Mifflin, 1979), 30–36.

110. See Jonah and Lawson, "Effectiveness of the Canadian Mandatory Seat Belt Use Law"; and Allan F. Williams, Adrian K. Lund, David F. Preusser, and Richard D. Blomberg, "Results of a Seat Belt Use Law Enforcement and Publicity Campaign in Elmira, New York," *Accident Analysis and Prevention* 19 (1987): 243–49.

## *CHAPTER 3. Research Design and Methodology*

1. Peter H. Rossi, James D. Wright, and Sonia R. Wright, "The Theory and Practice of Applied Social Research," *Evaluation Quarterly* 2 (1978): 171–91.

2. For a comprehensive treatment of quasi-experimental research designs, see Thomas D. Cook and Donald T. Campbell, *Quasi-Experimentation* (Boston: Houghton-Mifflin, 1979). The discussion of time-series research designs borrows heavily from chapter 5 of this source.

3. Ibid., chapter 2.

4. Donald T. Campbell and H. Laurence Ross, "The Connecticut Crackdown on Speeding: Time-Series Data in Quasi-Experimental Analysis," *Law and Society Review* 3 (1968): 33–53.

5. A good discussion of the multiple time-series design is found in Cook and Campbell, *Quasi-Experimentation,* 214–18.

6. Ibid., 218–21.

7. H. Laurence Ross, Donald T. Campbell, and Gene V. Glass, "Determining the Social Effects of a Legal Reform: The British 'Breathalyzer' Crackdown of 1967," *American Behavioral Scientist* 13 (1970): 493–509.

8. Alexander C. Wagenaar, *Alcohol, Young Drivers and Traffic Accidents* (Lexington, Mass.: Lexington, 1983), 41.

9. The data in this study have been gathered from the Fatal Accident Reporting System, U.S. Department of Transportation, National Highway Traffic Safety Administration; and the British Ministry of Transportation.

10. James B. Jacobs, *Drunk Driving: An American Dilemma* (Chicago: University of Chicago Press, 1989), 102.

11. Much of the traffic safety literature convincingly demonstrates that the opinions of police officers as to what constitutes an alcohol-related accident are too varied to be used. Not only do opinions vary, but reporting instruments vary. For a good discussion see Wagenaar, *Alcohol, Young Drivers and Traffic Accidents,* 42–43. See also E. Cerrelli, *Alcohol in Fatal Accidents National Estimates—USA* (Washington, D.C: U.S. Department of Transportation, National Highway Traffic Safety Administration, 1983); Timothy Heeren, Robert A. Smith, Suzette Morelock, and Ralph W. Hingson, "Surrogate Measures of Alcohol Involvement in Fatal Crashes: Are Conventional Indicators Adequate?" *Journal of Safety Research* 16 (1985): 127–34; and Pieter C. Noordzij, "Measuring the Extent of the Drinking and Driving Problem," *Accident Analysis and Prevention* 15 (1983): 407–14.

12. The data are available in *Highway Statistics* (Washington, D.C.: U.S. Department of Transportation, Federal Highway Administration, 1975–1988).

13. William Evans and John D. Graham, "Traffic Safety and the Business Cycle," *Alcohol, Drugs and Driving* 4 (1988): 31–38.

14. Cook and Campbell, *Quasi-Experimentation,* 228.

15. See G. E. P. Box and G. M. Jenkins, *Time Series Analysis: Forecasting and Control,* revised edition (San Francisco: Holden-Day, 1976); and G. E. P. Box and G. C. Tiao, "Intervention Analysis with

Applications to Economic and Environmental Problems," *Journal of the American Statistical Association* 70 (1975): 70–92. Other sources on time-series analysis include Leslie J. McCain and Richard McCleary, "The Statistical Analysis of the Simple Interrupted Time-Series Quasi-Experiment," in Cook and Campbell, *Quasi-Experimentation*, 223–93; and Richard McCleary and Richard A. Hay, Jr., *Applied Time Series Analysis for the Social Sciences* (Beverly Hills: Sage, 1980).

16. *SAS User's Guide: Econometrics and Time Series Laboratory* (Cary, N.C.: SAS Institute, 1982).

17. I tested for two models of change in the series: a temporary and a permanent impact. A *step* function suggests an immediate and permanent shift in a series and is coded 0 prior to the onset of a law and 1 afterward. A *pulse* function is indicative of temporary change and is coded 0 for all observations except the point of impact, where it is coded 1. Readers are urged to consult the above sources for a thorough understanding of ARIMA impact models.

18. While much statistical literature recommends eliminating insignificant parameters to improve specification, I include all interventions and control variables whether significant or not. The effects of policy may be better compared if the full models are included. I experimented with trimmed models, without achieving markedly different results, especially for reforms aimed at curbing alcohol-impaired driving.

## *CHAPTER 4. British Traffic Safety Reforms*

1. The term *Christmas Crusade* was coined by H. Laurence Ross, "Britain's Christmas Crusade Against Drinking and Driving," *Journal of Studies on Alcohol* 48 (1987): 476–82. My description of the crusade borrows heavily from Ross. Also, I am grateful to Professor Ross and the Department of Transportation for providing the data used in this chapter.

2. Ibid,; and Jerome S. Legge, Jr., "Reforming Public Safety: An Evaluation of the 1983 British Seat Belt Law," *Law and Policy* 9 (1987): 17–36; M. Mackay, "Seat Belt Use Under Voluntary and Mandatory Conditions and Its Effects on Casualties," in *Symposium on Human Behavior and Traffic Safety* (Warren, Mich.: General Motors

Research Laboratories, 1984), 259–83; and G. Pye and E. A. Waters, "Effect of Seat Belt Legislation on Injuries and Road Traffic Accidents in Nottingham," *British Journal of Medicine* 288 (1984): 756–57.

3. Howard Leichter, "Lives, Liberty, and Seat Belts in Britain: Lessons for the United States," *International Journal of Health Services* 16 (1986): 213–26.

4. Road Traffic Act (1972) 533A (3) para. 122.

5. "Belt Up or Regret It," *Sunday Times* (London), 30 January 1983.

6. John Coates, "Police in Two Minds on Seat Belt Law," *Sunday Times*, (London), 30 January 1983.

7. *Social Trends* 14, 18 (London: Her Majesty's Stationary Office, 1984, 1988); and Central Statistical Office, *Annual Abstract of Statistics* 119, 122 (London: Her Majesty's Stationary Office, 1985, 1986).

8. Coates, "Police in Two Minds on Seat Belt Law."

9. Ross, "Britain's Crusade," 481.

10. H. Laurence Ross, "Deterrence Regained: The Cheshire Constabulary's 'Breathalyzer Blitz,'" *Journal of Legal Studies* 6 (1977): 403–13. A number of American States have experimented with the blitz approach, with results similar to Cheshire's. In particular, see Robert B. Voas and Janet M. Hause, "Deterring the Drinking Driver: The Stockton Experience," *Accident Analysis and Prevention* 19 (1987): 81–90; H. Laurence Ross, "Deterring Drunken Driving: An Analysis of Current Efforts," *Journal of Studies on Alcohol*, Supplement 10 (1985): 122–28; Brian H. Jonah and R. Jean Wilson, "Improving the Effectiveness of Drinking-Driving Enforcement Through Increased Efficiency," *Accident Analysis and Prevention* 15 (1983): 463–81.

11. Paul M. Hurst, "Compulsory Seat Belt Use: Further Inferences," *Accident Analysis and Prevention* 11 (1979): 27–33.

12. Ibid., 27.

13. M. H. Cameron, "The Effect of Seat Belts on Minor and Severe Injuries Measured on the Abbreviated Injury Scale," *Accident Analysis and Prevention* 13 (1981): 17–25.

14. Brian A. Jonah and John J. Lawson, "The Effectiveness of the Canadian Mandatory Seat Belt Use Laws," *Accident Analysis and Prevention* 16 (1984): 433–50.

15. "Canada Credits High Belt Use Rates to Publicity, Enforcement" *Status Report* 23 (1988) (Insurance Institute for Highway

Safety), 1; Brian A. Jonah and Nancy E. Dawson, "Predicting Reported Seat Belt Use from Attitudinal and Normative Factors," *Accident Analysis and Prevention* 14 (1982): 305–09; R. A. Warren and H. M. Simpson, *Seat Belts and Traffic Safety: A Review of the Canadian Experience* (Ottawa: Traffic Injury Research Foundation of Canada, 1980); and Michael E. Matthews, "Seat Belt Use in Ontario Four Years After Mandating Legislation," *Accident Analysis and Prevention* 14 (1982): 431–38.

16. Connie M. Kristiansen, "Seat Belt Legislation and Seat Belt Use: Effects on Differences Related to Sex, Social Class and Smoking," *Accident Analysis and Prevention* 17 (1985): 75–78.

17. H. Laurence Ross, *Deterring the Drinking Driver,* revised and updated edition (Lexington, Mass.: Lexington, 1984), 9.

18. Ibid., 48–58. The most recent evidence from Canada and Australia demonstrates short-term effects. See Carolyn B. Liban, Evelyn R. Vingilis, and Holly Blefgen, "The Canadian Drinking-Driving Counter Measure Experience," *Accident Analysis and Prevention* 19 (1987): 159–81; and Ross J. Homel, *Policing the Drinking Driver: Random Breath Testing and the Process of Deterrence* (Canberra, Australia: Federal Office of Road Safety, 1986).

19. Central Statistical Office, *Annual Abstract of Statistics,* 1985.

20. Thomas D. Cook and Donald T. Campbell, *Quasi-Experimentation* (Boston: Houghton-Mifflin, 1979), 214–21.

21. ARIMA models fit a $(p,d,q)$ $(P,D,Q)$ form, where $p$ = the number of autoregressive parameters in the model, $q$ = the number of moving average parameters, and $d$ = the number of times a series must be differenced to achieve stationarity. $P$, $D$, and $Q$ are corresponding seasonal parameters. All models fit an ARIMA (1, 0, 0) (1, 0, 0) model except for the single-vehicle fatalities on weekend nights, which was (2, 1, 0) (1, 0, 0). Readers unfamiliar with the ARIMA technique may wish to consult the sources in chapter 3.

22. The problem of publicity as opposed to an intervention affecting behavior is discussed in Cook and Campbell, *Quasi- Experimentation,* 220–21; and H. Laurence Ross, "Law, Science and Accidents: The British Road Safety Act of 1967," *Journal of Legal Studies* 2 (1973): 1–78.

23. Cook and Campbell, *Quasi-Experimentation,* 218–21; Ross, *Deterring the Drinking Driver.* See also Leonard Evans and Michael C.

Frick, "Safety Belt Effectiveness in Preventing Driver Fatalities Versus a Number of Vehicular, Accident, Roadway and Environmental Factors," *Journal of Safety Research* 17 (1986): 143–54.

24. Central Statistical Office, *Annual Abstract of Statistics,* 1985, 193.

25. Ibid., 1988, 191.

26. Ibid., 196.

27. Ibid., 1986, 174.

28. Ibid., 1985, 111.

29. Ibid., 1986, 198.

30. H. Laurence Ross, "Final Report of the Presidential Commission on Drunk Driving," *Accident Analysis and Prevention* 17 (1985): 199–201.

31. Alexander C. Wagenaar, *Alcohol, Young Drivers and Traffic Accidents* (Lexington, Mass.: Lexington, 1983), 42–44.

32. Data on this variable were available only through 1984.

33. Central Statistical Office, *Annual Abstract of Statistics,* 1986.

34. This finding agrees with Ross, "Britain's Crusade," 481.

35. Michael Baily, "Road Accident Deaths Down 12% since Seat Belts Made Compulsory in 1983," *The Times* (London), 7 August 1985.

36. Of course, the most recent effort by the federal government has been to force the states to raise the drinking age.

37. Ross, "Final Report on Drunk Driving."

38. James F. Mosher, "Alcohol Policy and the Presidential Commission on Drunk Driving: The Paths Not Taken," *Accident Analysis and Prevention* 17 (1985): 239–50; and Graeme A. Thomson, "Drinking and Driving Accident Countermeasures: Why Not Try Changing the Environment?" *Accident Analysis and Prevention* 17 (1985): 207–10.

39. Thomson, 210.

40. Franklin Zimring and Gordon Hawkins, "The Legal Threat as an Instrument of Social Change," *Journal of Social Issues* 39 (1983): 143–57.

## *CHAPTER 5. Highway Safety in New York State*

1. "Carey Opens Fight on Drunken Driving," *New York Times,* 10 December 1979, section D.

2. "State Raises Penalties for Drivers Impaired by Drinking or Drugs," *New York Times,* 30 July 1980, section B.

3. "Carey Signs Bill to Aid Police in Curbing Drunken Drivers," *New York Times,* 15 July 1982, section B.

4. "Carey Signs Bill Revoking License for a 2nd Impaired Driving Offense," *New York Times,* 4 August 1982, section B.

5. Susan Chira, "Legislators Promote Restitution for Crime Victims," *New York Times,* 19 July 1983.

6. "Carey Signs a 4-Bill Drunken Driving Package," *New York Times,* 9 August 1981.

7. Phyllis Bernstein, "Drunken Driving Deaths Fall," *New York Times,* 5 January 1986, section 21.

8. Ibid. 19

9. *Crime and Criminal Justice Annual Report* (Albany, N.Y.: Executive Department, 1980–1983).

10. James Brooke, "Drunken Driving Fatalities Declining," *New York Times,* 27 August 1986, section B.

11. A. T. McCarrtt and A. M. Dowling, *An Impact Evaluation of the New York State STOP-DWI Program* (Albany, N.Y.: Institute for Traffic Safety Management and Research, 1985).

12. Brooks, "Drunken Driving Fatalities Declining."

13. Clifford D. May, "Rise in Legal Drinking Age Starts Amid Hope and Some Skepticism," *New York Times,* 30 November 1985.

14. Ibid.

15. "Governor Says Deaths Decline with New Law," *New York Times,* 26 April 1986, section B.

16. Timothy P. Williams and Robert P. Lillis, "Changes in Alcohol Consumption by 18-Year-Olds Following an Increase in New York State's Purchase Age to 19," *Journal of Studies on Alcohol* 47 (1986): 290–96.

17. Highway Safety Research Center, *1985–1986 Experience with Belt Laws in the United States* (Chapel Hill: University of North Carolina, 1987), 2. The primary source for these data are D. H. Rood, P. P. Kraichy, and A. T. McCarrtt, *Evaluation of New York State's Mandatory Occupant Restraint Law, Vol. 6—Final Summary Report* (Albany, N.Y.: Institute for Traffic Safety Management and Research, 1987).

18. D. H. Rood, P. P. Kraichy, and J. Carubia, *Evaluation of New York State's Mandatory Occupant Restraint Law: Observational Survey of*

*Restraint Use in New York State: April 1985* (Albany, N.Y.: Institute for Traffic Safety Management and Research, 1985).

19. A. T. McCarrtt, A. M. Dowling, and D. H. Rood, *Evaluation of New York's Mandatory Occupant Restraint Law, Vol. 5 Fatalities and Injuries Among Motor Vehicle Occupants Covered by the Law* Washington, D.C.: National Highway Traffic Safety Administration, 1987). Other evaluations are in the same general range. For example, see Adrian K. Lund, Jessica Pollner, and Allan F. Williams, "Preliminary Estimates of the Effects of Mandatory Seat Belt Use Laws," *Accident Analysis and Prevention* 19 (1987): 219–23; and Eric A. Latimer and Lester B. Lave, "Initial Effects of the New York State Auto Safety Belt Law," *American Journal of Public Health* 77 (1987): 183–86.

20. Robert D. McFadden, "Deaths on State Highways Decline to Lowest Level Since '49," *New York Times,* 18 May 1986.

21. In the end, because of the strength of the DWI reform, all interventions were tested for permanent change using a step function. See the appendix for the model impacts.

22. The ARIMA models identified and estimated are as follows:

| *Series* | *Model* | |
|---|---|---|
| All Fatalities | (0, 0, 0) | (1, 1, 0) |
| Single-vehicle fatalities, males, nighttime | (0, 0, 0) | (2, 1, 0) |
| Single-vehicle fatalities, all drivers, daytime | (0, 0, 0) | (1, 1, 0) |
| Single- and multiple-vehicle fatalities, all drivers, daytime | (0, 0, 0) | (1, 0, 0) |
| Front seat passengers | (0, 0, 0) | (1, 1, 0) |
| Back seat passengers | (1, 0, 0) | (1, 0, 0) |

For a more technical treatment of this material, see Jerome S. Legge, Jr., "Reforming Traffic Safety in New York State: The Effects of Alternative Policy Interventions," *Social Science Quarterly* 71 (1990): 373–82.

23. This interpretation is consistent with the one made by McCarrtt, Dowling, and Rood, *Fatalities and Injuries*, 21.

24. Rood, Kraichy, and Carubia, *Observational Survey of Restraint Use*.

25. Allan F. Williams, Adrian K. Lund, and David F. Preusser, "Teenage Driver Licensing in Relation to State Laws," *Accident Analysis and Prevention* 17 (1985): 135–45.

26. David F. Preusser, Allan F. Williams, and Adrian K. Lund, "Night Driving Curfews in New York and Louisiana: Results of a Questionnaire Survey," *Accident Analysis and Prevention* 17 (1985): 461–66.

27. David F. Preusser, Allan F. Williams, Paul L. Zador, and Richard D. Blomberg, "The Effect of Curfew Laws on Motor Vehicle Crashes," *Law and Policy Quarterly* 6 (1984): 115–28.

28. The increase in miles driven is probably the most important factor. Actually, the DWI parameters are not markedly different through 1987 compared to 1986.

29. *Annual Statistical Review* (Washington: Distilled Spirits Industry, 1983–1984), 37.

30. C. M. Kristiansen, "Seat Belt Legislation and Belt Use: Effect on Differences Related to Sex, Social Class, and Smoking," *Accident Analysis and Prevention* 17 (1985): 75–78; David F. Preusser, Adrian K. Lund, Allan F. Williams, and Richard D. Blomberg, "Belt Use by High-Risk Drivers Before and After New Year's Seat Belt Use Law," *Accident Analysis and Prevention* 20 (1988): 245–50.

31. David F. Preusser, Allan F. Williams, and Adrian K. Lund, "The Effect of New York's Seat Belt Use Law on Teenage Drivers," *Accident Analysis and Prevention* 19 (1987): 73–80.

32. A good start is B. J. Campbell and F. A. Campbell, *Seat Belt Experience in Four Foreign Countries Compared to the United States* (Falls Church, Va.: AAA Foundation for Traffic Safety, 1986). See also Robert N. Hayden, "Cultural Context and the Impact of Traffic Safety Legislation: The Reception of Mandatory Seat Belt Laws in Yugoslavia and Illinois," *Law and Society Review* 23 (1989): 283–94.

33. Alexander C. Wagenaar, *Alcohol, Young Drivers and Traffic Accidents* (Lexington, Mass.: Lexington, 1983).

## *CHAPTER 6. California*

1. Beverly Beyette, "Mothers' Crusade to Get Drunk Drivers off the Streets," *Los Angeles Times,* 11 June 1981, section 5.

2. Ibid.

3. "The Loaded Weapon," *Los Angeles Times,* 29 March 1981, section 5.

4. Claudia Luther, "Panel Tries to Toughen Drunk Driver Penalties," *Los Angeles Times,* 24 February 1981, section 1.

5. Gaylord Shaw, "Justice Demanded by Drunk Driver Victims," *Los Angeles Times,* 3 November 1981, section 1.

6. Luther, "Tough Drunk Driver Penalties."

7. "Loaded Weapon."

8. Robert Fairbanks, "Brown Signs Tough Drunk Driving Bills," *Los Angeles Times,* 30 September 1981, section 1.

9. Ibid.

10. Ibid.

11. H. Laurence Ross, *Deterring the Drinking Driver,* revised and updated edition (Lexington, Mass.: Lexington, 1984), 119–20.

12. Gene Blake, "Drunk Driver Sentenced to 4½ Year Term," *Los Angeles Times,* 31 October 1981, section 1.

13. *Los Angeles Times,* 16 September 1981, section 1.

14. Kenneth Reich, "Mandatory Seat Belt Law Comes in with New Year," *Los Angeles Times,* 31 December 1985, section 1.

15. Highway Safety Research Center, *1985–1986 Experience with Belt Laws in the United States* (Chapel Hill: University of North Carolina, 1987), 2.

16. Sandy Banks, "Reiner Rejects New Drunk Driving Law," *Los Angeles Times,* 20 January 1982, section 2.

17. James E. Blatt, "Tightening Up on Drunks," letter to the editor, *Los Angeles Times,* 11 March 1981, section 2.

18. Sandy Banks, "Courts Struggle with Logjam of Drunk-Driving Cases," *Los Angeles Times,* 5 August 1982, section 2.

19. Sandy Banks, "Drunk-Driver Education for Indigents Seen as Dilemma," *Los Angeles Times,* 9 May 1983, section 1.

20. Ibid.

21. John O'Dell, "$200 Fee for Drunk Driver Class Creates Furor," *Los Angeles Times,* 1 March 1982, section 2.

22. Bob Baker, "D.A. Targets Scofflaws in Drunk-Driver Cases," *Los Angeles Times,* 29 October 1986, section 1.

23. *The California DUI Countermeasures System: An Evaluation of System Processing and Deficiencies* (Sacramento: California Department of Motor Vehicles Research and Development Office, 1986).

24. R. C. Peck, *The Traffic Safety Impact of California's New Drunk Driving Law (AB541): An Evaluation of the First Nine Months of Experience* Sacramento: California Department of Motor Vehicles, 1983).

25. Michael E. Hilton, "The Impact of Recent Changes in California Drinking-Driving Laws on Fatal Accident Levels During the First Postintervention Year: An Interrupted Time Series Analysis," *Law and Society Review* 18 (1984): 605–27. I find a stronger reduction than Hilton does for the first year. The reason for the difference may rest with my unit of analysis being the fatality rather than the fatal accident.

26. Sam Enriquez, "Glendale Enforcing Seat Belt Law—Deaths, Injuries Down," *Los Angeles Times,* 10 February 1986, section 2.

27. The ARIMA models for the California series are as follows. (See the appendix for the estimates of these models.)

| *Series* | *Model* |
|---|---|
| All fatalities | (0, 1, 1) (0, 1, 1) |
| Single-vehicle fatalities, males, nighttime | (0, 0, 0) (0, 0, 1) |
| Single-vehicle fatalities, all drivers, daytime | (0, 1, 0) (0, 1, 1) |
| Single- and multiple-vehicle fatalities, all drivers, daytime | (0, 1, 1) (0, 1, 1) |
| Front seat passengers | (0, 1, 1) (0, 0, 1) |
| Back seat passengers | (0, 0, 0) (0, 1, 1) |
| All fatalities, under age 21 | (0, 0, 0) (0, 0, 0) |
| Single-vehicle fatalities, drivers under age 21, nighttime | (0, 0, 2) (0, 0, 1) |

28. Jerome S. Legge, Jr., "Reforming Public Safety: An Evalua-

tion of the 1983 British Seat Belt Law," *Law and Policy* 9 (1987): 17–36.

29. William R. Stevens, "Deaths from Drunken Driving Increase," *New York Times,* 29 October 1987.

30. California Department of Justice, *Crime and Deliquency in California* (Sacramento, Calif.: California Dept. of Justice, 1987).

31. Ross, *Deterring the Drinking Driver,* 119–20.

## *CHAPTER 7. Michigan*

1. Alexander C. Wagenaar, "Preventing Highway Crashes by Raising the Legal Minimum Age for Drinking: The Michigan Experience Six Years Later," *Journal of Safety Research* 17 (1986): 101–09.

2. R. Douglass and J. Freedman, *Alcohol-Related Casualties and Alcohol Beverage Market Response to Beverage Alcohol Availability Policies in Michigan* (Ann Arbor: University of Michigan Highway Safety Research Institute, 1977).

3. Julie Morris and Glen Weingarten, "Bars Rally Youth Drinking Vote," *Detroit Free Press,* 20 September 1978 (*Newsbank,* Law and Order, 112: B10-B12).

4. Jerry Moskal, "Under 21 Drinkers Just Changed Style to Accommodate Law," *State Journal,* 26 January 1979 (*Newsbank,* Law and Order, 11: 614-12A1).

5. Morris and Weingarten, "Bars Rally Youth Drinking Vote."

6. Jerry Moskal, "21 Drinking Age Faces Legal Test," *State Journal,* 15 November 1978 (*Newsbank,* Law and Order, 126: B13).

7. Moskal, "Under 21 Drinkers Just Changed Style."

8. Morris and Weingarten, "Bars Rally Youth Drinking Vote."

9. John Askins, "Students Register to Vote to Drink," *Detroit Free Press,* 13 October 1978 (*Newsbank,* Law and Order, 112: B9).

10. Steve Burzynski, "'D' Tough on Bar Owners," *State Journal,* 9 November 1978 (*Newsbank,* Law and Order, 122: 613).

11. Polk Laffoon, "Suit Challenges No Drinking-Till-21 Law," *Detroit Free Press,* 28 November 1978 (*Newsbank,* Law and Order, 132: 68).

12. Ibid.

13. Tim McCormack and Tom Rademacher, "Tavern Doors Shut

on Under-21 Drinkers," *Grand Rapids Press*, 23 December 1978 (*Newsbank*, Law and Order, 132: 613-14).

14. Ibid.

15. Moskal, "Under 21 Drinkers."

16. Ibid.

17. Sue Burzynski, "Bars Using Hand Stamps," *State Journal*, 7 January 1979 (*Newsbank*, Law and Order, 4: A6).

18. Paul Magnasson, "Youth Can Still Drink, 21 or No, in Many Bars," *Detroit Free Press*, 31 December 1978 (*Newsbank*, Law and Order, 132: 610-11).

19. Chris Meehan, "Mansma Seeks Tough Drink-Drive Penalties," *Grand Rapids Press*, 24 March 1982 (*Newsbank*, TRA28: D8).

20. Jerry Morlock, "Tougher Drunk-Driver Law Starts in State Wednesday," *Grand Rapids Press*, 27 March 1983 (*Newsbank*, TRA23: 612). This chapter's description of the new law is based on this article.

21. Jerry Morlock, "System Weakens Drunk Driving Law, Study Says," *Grand Rapids Press*, 4 June 1984 (*Newsbank*, TRA34: A1).

22. Morlock, "Tougher Drunk-Driver Law."

23. Morlock, "System Weakens Drunk Driving Law."

24. Michigan Department of State Police, *Michigan Traffic Accident Facts, 1984* (Lansing: Dept. of State Police, 1986), 17.

25. Ron D. Wonkowski, "Seat Belts Unbuckled in 90% of Car Deaths," *Detroit Free Press*, 11 January 1985 (*Newsbank*, CON: B3).

26. Ibid.

27. Ron D. Wonkowski, "Mandatory Seat Belt Bill Passes," *Detroit Free Press*, 20 February 1985 (*Newsbank*, CON4: B14-C2).

28. Wonkowski, "Seat Belts Unbuckled."

29. Chris Golembiewski, "Better Start Buckling Up—Few Get Seat Belts Waived," *State Journal*, 3 June 1985 (*Newsbank*, CON20: D1).

30. Wonkowski, "Mandatory Seat Belt Bill Passes."

31. Ibid.

32. Golembiewski, "Better Start Buckling Up."

33. Highway Safety Research Center, *1985–86 Experience with Seat Belt Laws in the United States* (Chapel Hill: University of North Carolina, 1987), 3–4.

34. Roddy Ray, "New Law Gets Twice as Many to Buckle Up," *Detroit Free Press*, 7 July 1985, (*Newsbank*, CON25: B9–10).

35. Susan Goldberg, "Seat Belts Great—for Others," *Detroit Free Press*, 31 December 1985 (*Newsbank*, CON44: C7).

36. Alexander C. Wagenaar, Lisa J. Molnar, and Karen L. Businski, *Direct Observation of Seat Belt Use in Michigan* (Ann Arbor: University of Michigan Transportation Research Institute, 1988), 13. See also Alexander C. Wagenaar and Margaret B. T. Wiviott, "Effect of Mandating Seat Belt Use: A Series of Surveys on Compliance in Michigan," *Public Health Reports* 101 (1986): 505–13.

37. Ibid.

38. The Michigan models were consistent in that there is considerable seasonality in the data. In addition, the variance in observations is inconsistent across time. Logarithmic transformation was attempted first, but it did not improve the noise component of the series substantially. In some cases the fit of the model worsened. In the end, it was necessary to difference each series seasonally to determine program impact. The ARIMA models identified and estimated for the series are as follows:

| *Series* | *Model* | |
|---|---|---|
| All fatalities | (1, 0, 0) | (0, 1, 1) |
| Single-vehicle fatalities, males, nighttime | (0, 0, 0) | (0, 1, 1) |
| Single-vehicle fatalities, all drivers, daytime | (0, 0, 0) | (0, 1, 1) |
| Single- and multiple-vehicle fatalities, all drivers, daytime | (0, 0, 0) | (0, 1, 1) |
| Front seat passengers | (0, 0, 0) | (0, 1, 1) |
| Back seat passengers | (0, 0, 0) | (0, 1, 1) |
| All fatalities, under age 21 | (0, 0, 0) | (0, 1, 1) |
| Single-vehicle fatalities, male drivers under age 21 | (0, 0, 0) | (0, 1, 1) |
| All fatalities, driver age 21 | (0, 0, 0) | (0, 1, 1) |

The model for all fatalities was unusual in that it contained both moving average and autoregressive components. Exponential decay was evident in both the autocorrelation and partial autocorrelation functions, indicating this possibility. More conservative models were tried, eliminating either the moving average or the autoregressive component. While the program impacts were similar, I was not able to obtain white noise in the residuals unless the additional component of the model was added. Also see the appendix for the estimates.

39. Alexander C. Wagenaar, *Alcohol, Young Drivers and Traffic Accidents* (Lexington, Mass.: Lexington, 1983), 45–46.

40. Wagenaar, Molnar, and Businski, *Direct Observation,* 13.

41. As in California, reductions were evident if youthful drivers were analyzed in the night hours. However, the number of cases was low; I am more confident if all single-vehicle fatalities are used.

42. See, for example Peter Asch and David T. Levy, "Does the Minimum Drinking Age Affect Traffic Fatalities?" *Journal of Policy Analysis and Management* 6 (1987): 180–92.

43. Alexander C. Wagenaar, Frederic M. Streff, and Robert H. Schultz, "The Effects of the 65 MPH Speed Limit on Injury, Morbidity, and Mortality," *Accident Analysis and Prevention* 22 (1990): 571–85.

44. Wagenaar, *Alcohol, Young Drivers and Traffic Accidents.*

45. H. Laurence Ross, "Administrative License Revocation in New Mexico: An Evaluation," *Law and Policy* 9 (1987): 5–16.

46. Wagenaar, Molnar, and Businski, *Direct Observation;* and Wagenaar and Wiviott, "Effects of Mandating Seat Belt Use," 509.

47. These results are in agreement with the UMTRI analysis regarding fatalities in response to the seat belt law. While the UMTRI did find a decline in fatalities, the drop was not significant. The Michigan researchers attribute the lack of significance to the lower population of fatalities as opposed to injuries and the short time span they used following the law's implementation. Further, the UMTRI demonstrated an impressive reduction in injuries due to the effect of the seat belt law. Analysis of injuries is beyond the scope of this book. See Alexander C. Wagenaar, Richard G. Maybee, and Kathleen P. Sullivan, *Michigan's Compulsory Restraint Use Policies: Effects on Injuries and Deaths* (Ann Arbor: University of Michigan Transportation Re-

search Institute, 1987), and Fredrick M. Streff, Alexander C. Wagenaar, and Robert H. Schultz, "Reductions in Police-Reported Injuries Associated with Michigan's Safety Belt Law," *Journal of Safety Research* 21 (1990): 9–18.

## CHAPTER 8. *Implications for Public Policy*

1. Franklin E. Zimring, "Law, Society and the Drinking Driver: Some Concluding Reflections," in *Social Control of the Drinking Driver*, ed. Michael D. Laurence, John R. Snortum, and Franklin E. Zimring (Chicago: University of Chicago Press, 1988), 218.

2. John R. Snortum, "Deterrence of Alcohol-Impaired Driving: An Effect in Search of a Cause," in *Social Control of the Drinking Driver*, 218.

3. Joseph R. Gusfield, "The Control of Drinking-Driving in the United States: A Period of Transition?" in *Social Control of the Drinking Driver*, 133.

4. H. Laurence Ross, Hans Klette, and Richard McCleary, "Liberalization and Rationalization of Drunk-Driving Laws in Scandinavia," *Accident Analysis and Prevention* 16 (1984): 471–87.

5. James B. Jacobs, *Drunk Driving: An American Dilemma* (Chicago: University of Chicago Press, 1989), 119–20.

6. Snortum, "Deterrence of Alcohol-Impaired Driving," 209–13.

7. Jacobs, *Drunk Driving*, 71.

8. For the most recent research on speed limits, see Herbert M. Baum, Jo Ann K. Wells, and Adrian K. Lund, "Motor Vehicle Crash Fatalities in the Second Year of 65 MPH Speed Limits," *Journal of Safety Research* 21 (1990): 1–8; and Steve Garber and John D. Graham, "The Effect of the New 65 Miles-per-Hour Speed Limit on Rural Highway Fatalities: A State-by-State Analysis," *Accident Analysis and Prevention* 22 (1990): 137–49.

9. Paul Wasielewski, "Speed as a Measure of Accident Risk: Observed Speeds Versus Driver and Vehicle Characteristics," *Accident Analysis and Prevention* 16 (1984): 89–103.

10. A recent study using data gathered from medical records in Illinois underscores the fact that, while the benefits of present compliance are great, more potential can be realized through greater seat belt use. See Elizabeth Mueller Orsay et al., "Prospective Study of the

Effect of Safety Belts on Morbidity and Health Care Costs in Motor Vehicle Accidents," *Journal of the American Medical Association* 260 (1988): 3598–603; see also Terrence L. Chorba, Donald Reinfurt, and Barbara J. Hulka, "Effect of Mandatory Seat-Belt Use Legislation: The North Carolina Experience from 1983 through 1987," *Journal of the American Medical Association* 260 (1988): 3593–97.

11. A recent and very useful study by Robert N. Hayden uses culture and regard for the law in explaining differences in compliance between Yugoslavia and Illinois. In Yugoslavia, compliance is much lower than in the United States despite strong government attempts to enforce the law. See "Cultural Context and the Impact of Traffic Safety Legislation: The Reception of Mandatory Seat Belt Laws in Yugoslavia and Illinois," *Law and Society Review* 23 (1989): 283–94.

12. The potential of insurance as a deterrent to alcohol-related crashes has its limitations. See James B. Jacobs, "The Impact of Insurance and Civil Law Sanctions on Drunk Driving," in *Social Control of the Drinking Driver*, 227–47.

13. See Snortum, "Deterrence of Alcohol-Impaired Driving," 204–21.

14. See Robert P. Voas, "Emerging Technologies for Controlling the Drunk Driver," in *Social Control of the Drinking Driver*, 270–94.

# INDEX

*PITT SERIES IN POLICY AND INSTITUTIONAL STUDIES*

Bert A. Rockman, Editor

*The Acid Rain Controversy*
James L. Regens and Robert W. Rycroft

*Affirmative Action at Work: Law, Politics, and Ethics*
Bron Raymond Taylor

*Agency Merger and Bureaucratic Redesign*
Karen M. Hult

*The Aging: A Guide to Public Policy*
Bennett M. Rich and Martha Baum

*Arms for the Horn: U.S. Security Policy in Ethiopia and Somalia, 1953–1991*
Jeffrey A. Lefebvre

*The Atlantic Alliance and the Middle East*
Joseph I. Coffey and Gianni Bonvicini, Editors

*The Budget-Maximizing Bureaucrat: Appraisals and Evidence*
André Blais and Stéphane Dion

*Clean Air: The Policies and Politics of Pollution Control*
Charles O. Jones

*The Competitive City: The Political Economy of Suburbia*
Mark Schneider

*Conflict and Rhetoric in French Policymaking*
Frank R. Baumgartner

*Congress and Economic Policymaking*
Darrell M. West

*Congress Oversees the Bureaucracy: Studies in Legislative Supervision*
Morris S. Ogul

*Democracy in Japan*
Takeshi Ishida and Ellis S. Krauss, Editors

*Demographic Change and the American Future*
R. Scott Fosler, William Alonso, Jack A. Meyer, and Rosemary Kern

*Economic Decline and Political Change: Canada, Great Britain, and the United States*
Harold D. Clarke, Marianne C. Stewart, and Gary Zuk, Editors

*Extraordinary Measures: The Exercise of Prerogative Powers in the United States*
Daniel P. Franklin

*Foreign Policy Motivation: A General Theory and a Case Study*
Richard W. Cottam

*"He Shall Not Pass This Way Again": The Legacy of Justice William O. Douglas*
Stephen L. Wasby, Editor

*Homeward Bound: Explaining Changes in Congressional Behavior*
Glenn Parker

*How Does Social Science Work? Reflections on Practice*
Paul Diesing

*Imagery and Ideology in U.S. Policy Toward Libya, 1969–1982*
Mahmoud G. ElWarfally

*The Impact of Policy Analysis*
James M. Rogers

*Iran and the United States: A Cold War Case Study*
Richard W. Cottam

*Japanese Prefectures and Policymaking*
Steven R. Reed

*Making Regulatory Policy*
Keith Hawkins and John M. Thomas, Editors

*Managing the Presidency: Carter, Reagan, and the Search for Executive Harmony*
Colin Campbell, S.J.

*Organizing Governance, Governing Organizations*
Colin Campbell, S.J., and B. Guy Peters, Editors

*Party Organizations in American Politics*
Cornelius P. Cotter et al.

*Perceptions and Behavior in Soviet Foreign Policy*
Richard K. Herrmann

*Pesticides and Politics: The Life Cycle of a Public Issue*
Christopher J. Bosso

*Policy Analysis by Design*
Davis B. Bobrow and John S. Dryzek

*The Political Failure of Employment Policy, 1945–1982*
Gary Mucciaroni

*Political Leadership: A Source Book*
Barbara Kellerman, Editor

*The Politics of Public Utility Regulation*
William T. Gormley, Jr.

*The Politics of the U.S. Cabinet: Representation in the Executive Branch, 1789–1984*
Jeffrey E. Cohen

*The Presidency and Public Policy Making*
George C. Edwards III, Steven A. Shull, and Norman C. Thomas, Editors

*Private Markets and Public Intervention: A Primer for Policy Designers*
Harvey Averch

*Public Policy in Latin America: A Comparative Survey*
John W. Sloan

*Roads to Reason: Transportation, Administration, and Rationality in Colombia*
Richard E. Hartwig

*Site Unseen: The Politics of Siting a Nuclear Waste Repository*
Gerald Jacob

*The Struggle for Social Security, 1900–1935*
Roy Lubove

*Tage Erlander: Serving the Welfare State, 1946–1969*
Olof Ruin

*Traffic Safety Reform in the United States and Great Britain*
Jerome S. Legge, Jr.

*Urban Alternatives: Public and Private Markets in the Provision of Local Services*
Robert M. Stein

*The U.S. Experiment in Social Medicine: The Community Health Center Program, 1965–1986*
Alice Sardell